Raising
Ricky

Raising Ricky

a memoir

A Sister's Lifetime Promise
to Protect Her Brother
with Down Syndrome

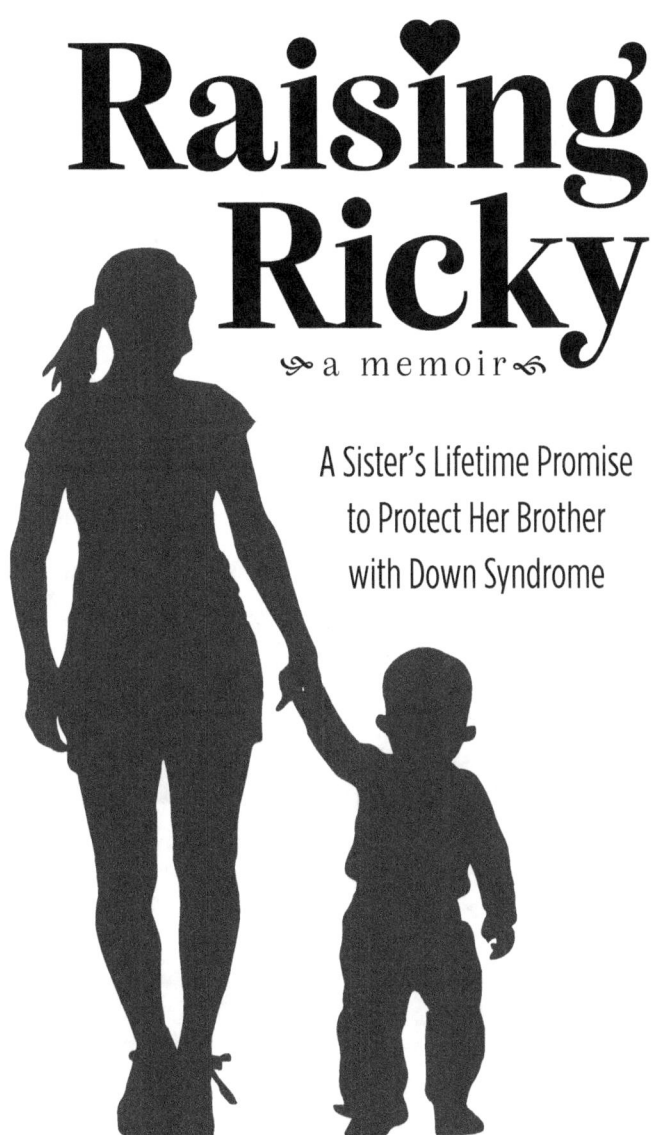

Debbie Miller

Raising Ricky: A Sister's Lifetime Promise to Protect Her Brother with Down Syndrome

For information about this title, contact the publisher:

Debbie Miller
authordebbiemiller@gmail.com
authordebbiemiller.com

Library of Congress Control Number: 2024925532

ISBNs:
979-8-9912486-0-0 (softcover)
979-8-9912486-1-7 (eBook)

Printed in the United States of America

Cover and Interior design: 1106 Design

Dedication

To my husband, who has walked every step of this journey
with me. He has been my rock and has always prioritized
the needs of my brother and me.
He is my partner, best friend, and my greatest supporter.
He is and will always be the one, who I love
more than life itself.

To my brother: I helped teach you many things,
but you taught me the true meaning of selfless, unconditional love.

To my daughters, whom I love more than they know.

To my grandsons—I am so very proud of the young men you are
and the great men you will become.

To my father and grandparents, who made my life worth living.
I hope I made you proud.

Acknowledgments

First, I need to acknowledge Amy Silverman for starting me on this writing journey after I took her creative writing class in Arizona more than twenty years ago. She gave me the validation that I had potential as a writer, and she introduced me to my developmental editor, Robrt Pela.

I'm grateful to Robrt for giving me the courage to write about difficult events and helping me become my authentic self. He knew how to improve my writing without changing my voice.

I need to thank Susie Baxter for her class, *Write Your Memoir,* for giving me the tools to bring my individual stories together as a cohesive manuscript.

I want to thank my Writers' Alliance of Gainesville (WAG) writing-pod members—Susie, Rachel, and Michele for their support and input regarding my writing and encouragement to publish.

I'm grateful to my beta readers: Gayle, Rosalind, Amy, Andrea, and Ellen. They gave me their honest input of what worked and what needed revision, and they supported our decisions regarding my brother.

I'm grateful for the support I received from my community book club. Especially Jen, who shared her Alzheimer's experience, and Lauren and Laurence, who helped getting Rick into the Fixel Institute.

I'm grateful to Amanda Sparkman's class, the Savvy Caregiver, which provided us a map and compass to navigate this uncharted dementia territory.

I'm thankful for my friend Kathryn Taubert for coming into my life when I needed her. Her Buddhist teachings helped me find peace with my childhood trauma and eased my guilt of meeting the needs of my husband and brother. She helped me more than any licensed therapist.

I am thankful to my cousin Trish, who stepped in for me during my mother's hospitalization and took care of my brother.

I must thank Nancy Eckburg. She has known my story since the beginning and has helped my family and me my entire life. I will be forever indebted to her. She may not be technically a family member, but in every sense of the word . . . she is family.

Lastly, I want to thank Michele, Ronda, and my team from 1106 Design for their collaboration in publishing my first book. They were absolutely wonderful to work with.

Disclaimer

This memoir is based on true events that reflect the author's present recollections of experiences over time. Names and characteristics of some individuals have been changed.

The conversations are from the author's memory, though not written in word-for-word transcripts, but retelling them in a way to evoke the feeling and meaning of what was said, and, in all instances, the essence of the dialogue is accurate.

The story is focused on the author's childhood with her brother and their later years, when faced with another difficult diagnosis.

Contents

Prologue
1959-1963, Illinois

I may have been a little spoiled before my brother was born. My mother sewed me the cutest dresses, even matching dresses for my doll, which made me the envy of my second-grade class.

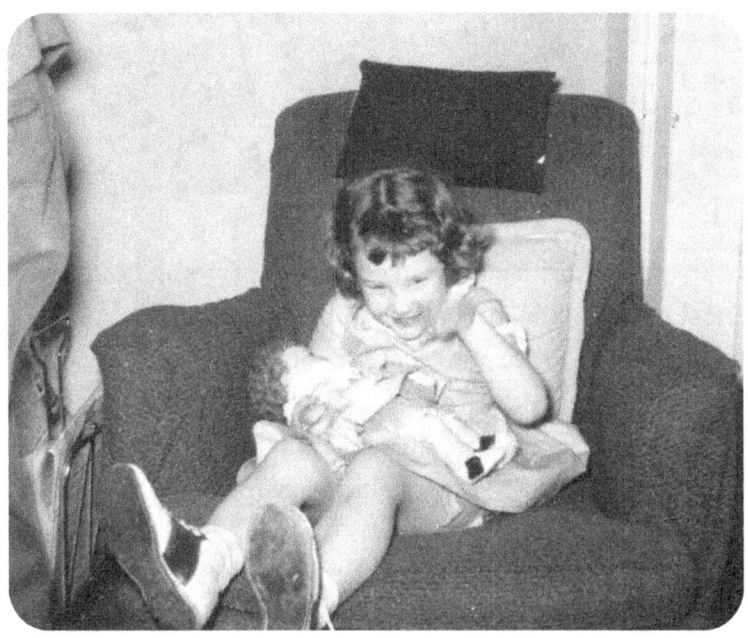

Daddy always had time to play board games and cards with me if it was raining or too cold to play outside.

We moved to the house on Fifth Street two years before my parents brought Ricky home. It was a two-story, but we lived on the first floor. It had a front living room that faced the street, a dining room, two bedrooms, a kitchen with an eating area, and one bathroom. The best part was the garage built into the hill at the back of the house, with steps on one side and a cement ramp on the other. All the kids in the neighborhood loved to play in our backyard, especially in the winter, because we had the best hill and ramp to sled on. Daddy enjoyed playing outside with the kids. Our yard was perfect for creating imaginary and mythical lands; my friends and I took turns playing the Queen or the Princess.

One day, when I arrived home from school, Daddy's car was already in the driveway. My parents were in my bedroom, moving all my things out, and putting a bunk bed together.

"What is going on? What are you doing with my dolls and toys?" I screamed at them.

"It's OK, honey," my dad said. "We're just rearranging things for your brother. You're going to share your room with him. He's getting too big for his crib." Ever since he'd been born, Ricky had slept in my parents' bedroom.

"No!" I stamped my feet. "This is not fair. I can't share a room with a boy." I started crying.

"That's enough," my father sternly responded to my tantrum. "You need to be nice and a good sister."

That's when my life changed. I loved my baby brother, but I didn't want to share my room and listen to his hissing vaporizer every night.

Soon, I would discover just how much my life was not my own. But I would also learn life's greatest lessons.

"To understand the value of life, one must learn the art of putting others first."

—Anonymous

Chapter One

Little Debbie's Brother
1964, Illinois

It was a sunny, warm day in early fall, and I was playing jump rope with my friends Barb and Jody on the school playground. "Your brother is a retard." The words seemed to come out of nowhere, like a gust of wind pushing me off balance.

I turned toward the voice. There was Linda, standing alone, with her hands on her hips and that familiar smirk on her face. I didn't like her very much. She was always picking on me and making fun of my clothes. Mostly, I ignored her. She had no friends to play with, and I had lots. But her daddy had the shiniest, biggest car I had ever seen, and she had the prettiest store-bought dresses.

I mainly wore hand-me-down clothes from my cousin, JoAnn. They didn't fit very well, because she was a chubby girl. Mom used to sew my dresses and sometimes would make a matching dress for my Tiny Tears doll. Even Linda was jealous of them. But that was before my brother was born. Mom didn't have much time for sewing anymore—or anything else except caring for Ricky.

Linda said it again. "Your brother is a retard. My mother said so."

What was that word I'd never heard before? I thought to myself. I knew it couldn't be nice, not with Linda saying it. And it was the way she said it—taunting me.

I wished I could come up with something clever to say, but all I could think of was, "He is not!"

"Everybody knows it," she yelled back. "He should go to the State Hospital, with all the other retards."

What was she talking about? Was Ricky sick? He did get a lot of colds, which is why he had to have the loud, smelly vaporizer hissing in our room every night.

I couldn't take it any longer. It was one thing when Linda made fun of *me*, but this was my little brother. I threw all my fury at her, pushing her down and screaming, "Take it back! Take it back!"

Mrs. Hitchcock, my fifth-grade teacher, an overweight woman with frizzy hair and a mole on her face, pulled me off Linda. Her bad breath smelled like onions and coffee.

"Debbie, I will not tolerate any fighting. You need to apologize."

"But she started it," I pleaded. "She called my brother a bad name."

"You should talk to your parents about that."

That didn't make any sense. *Why wasn't Linda in trouble?*

As I walked home from school, I thought about what the word "retard" could mean. Ricky did seem different. My friend Jody had a three-old-sister who could do all sorts of things that Ricky couldn't do.

Once, I asked Mom, "Why can Jill talk so much better than Ricky?" Even though he was also three, he still babbled baby talk and had just started walking a few months ago. She explained that girls matured faster and convinced me he would catch up soon. Her answer seemed reasonable when I considered the boys in my class. I remembered another time I heard Mom crying in her bedroom and Daddy consoling her. Since Ricky was born, Mom cried a lot, and she and Daddy quarreled more than ever. Everything changed . . . and not for the better.

"It will be all right," I heard him say. "We can take care of him."

"But what about Debbie? I don't have any time for her."

"She'll be fine; it'll make her stronger," Daddy replied.

By the time I reached my house, my mind was so cluttered with questions and thoughts that, as soon as I saw Mom, I blurted out, "Is Ricky a retard?"

Her shocked look of disgust was my first clue that I had said something terribly wrong. After her slap swept across my face, I knew for sure.

I ran to my room, sobbing, confused and scared. After Daddy got home from work, my parents came into my room.

"I'm sorry I slapped you."

Mom reached for me, but I pulled away, still afraid. She explained, "Ricky has a condition called Down syndrome. It means it will take him a little longer to learn things."

They promised he would learn everything sooner or later. But Mom cautioned me that not everyone agreed with them.

"Before we brought your baby brother home from the hospital, the doctor advised us to place him in an institution for disabled children. His prognosis was not good. He felt that Ricky might not *ever* talk—or even walk."

There were tears in her eyes.

"But we're devoted to giving Ricky a wonderful life," Daddy said. "He's our son and your brother. People might say mean things or give him funny looks. You will have to be very strong. Do you remember when we took Ricky to see Dr. McGlothin at the new clinic? He explained that Ricky had floppy muscles and that we could improve his strength with exercises. All of us worked with him—and you, most of all. We helped him raise his head and learn to roll over, sit up, and crawl. And now he's walking."

Little did I realize that I had become my brother's physical therapist, starting when I was seven.

Little Debbie's Brother

"I understand, and I'll help more. I'll help teach Ricky things," I told my parents. Later that night, I crawled into his lower bunk and held him close. I promised him and God that I would never let anyone hurt him. It was quite a lofty resolution for a ten-year-old. But I had to protect him; he was my brother.

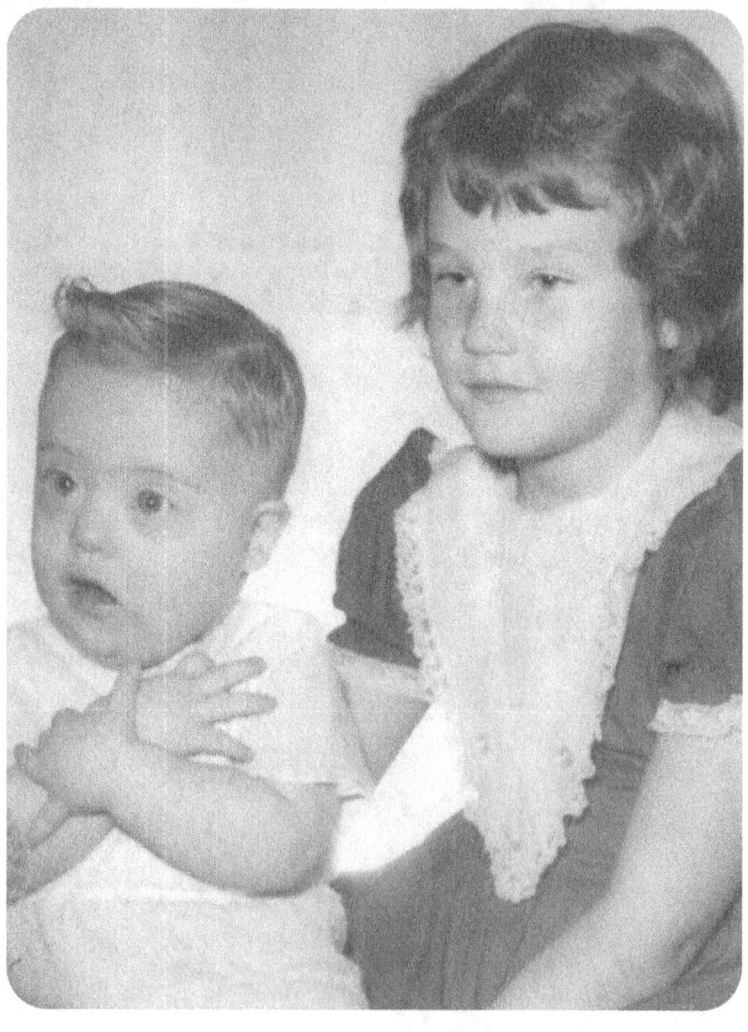

Things did change a little after that day. Dad became my rock. Mom grew sadder and more tired. She took a lot of naps. I wished my mother was more like my friends' mothers. She had red hair like Lucille Ball and a model's figure, which she liked to show off. In the summer, she would parade around in really short shorts and a shirt she'd tie under her chest to show off her midriff. It was so embarrassing.

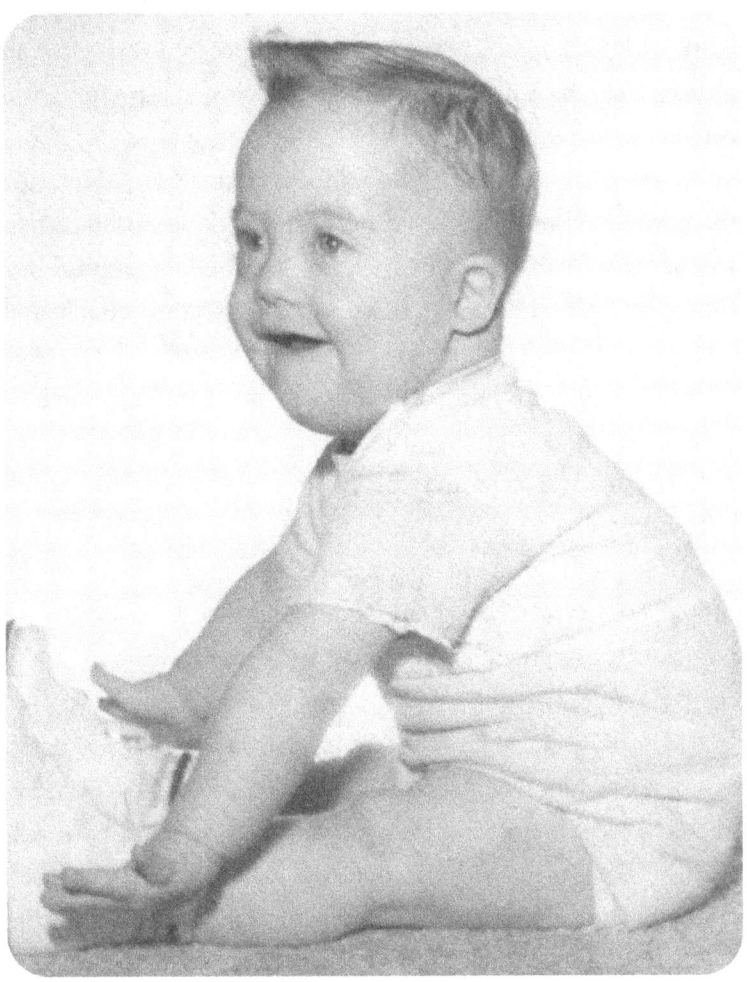

After Ricky was born, she changed and became less flamboyant. It was like she had become a different person. After my parents explained why my brother was special, things got worse. I tried my best to assist with the household chores, care for Ricky, and help him do his exercises. But, no matter what I did, it wasn't enough to fix my struggling family. I would rush home from school daily to straighten up the house and wash the dishes before Daddy came home from work. Then, I would work with Ricky on his exercises and his speech. I was so proud of him when he said his first word, "Dabby"—clear enough to understand that he meant "Debbie."

Mom said, "Of course, he said *your* name first." Her curt tone confused me. It seemed nothing I did ever pleased her. But at least Daddy noticed, and that was good enough for me. One day, when I got home, Mom was asleep on the couch, and Ricky was playing in his playpen, sitting in a soiled diaper. He started clapping his hands when he saw me, babbling, "Dabby, Dabby." I quickly changed his soaked diaper; I noticed his red bottom, and I wondered if Mom had changed him at all that day.

A car pulled into the driveway; I was surprised to see the unexpected visitor was Daddy. *Why was he home so early?* I panicked, not knowing what to do; I hadn't had time to do my "usual" chores.

He walked into the living room; his face had a disgusted expression I had never seen before as he looked at Mom. He picked up the empty bottle on the coffee table and threw it angrily into the trash. I watched him sit down at the kitchen counter, holding his head with his hands, his body shaking. *Was he crying?*

Feeling like a failure, I just sat there, holding my brother. Despite my best efforts, trying to be a good girl, doing the household work, and caring for Ricky, my family was still falling apart, and I didn't know how to fix it.

"Oh, you're home," Mom said to Dad. She was groggy and was slurring her words.

"Just go to bed, Mavis," Dad answered crossly.

Daddy made dinner, and we ate in silence; I had learned when to be quiet. While he cleaned up the kitchen, I bathed Ricky and put him to bed.

"Wuv you, Dabby," Ricky exclaimed, hugging me.

"I love you, too, Sweetie." Exhausted, I went to bed, too, thankful that tomorrow was Saturday and that Daddy would be home.

Waking up to my brother's chatter, I quickly dressed and looked for my father. Maybe we could do something fun today. It had been a long time since he had taken me to the park. But he was nowhere to be found. Mom was still in her bathrobe, sitting at the kitchen table, sipping coffee, staring out the window. Slowly, I approached her.

"Where's Dad?"

"At work—where else?" She sounded annoyed.

"But it's Saturday," I pleaded.

"Well, I guess you should talk to him about that. He doesn't seem to care what I think." I wanted to say something about last night but decided it would not be in my best interests, considering the slap from the other day and her current mood.

The doorbell rang, and I was relieved to see Aunt Nina on the porch. She rushed by me, straight to my mother, and hugged her before sitting down. Aunt Nina told me to go into the living room and watch TV with Ricky. Turning down the volume just a tad, I could hear parts of their conversation.

"Mavis, what the hell is going on with you? You'd better get your shit together and start taking care of your children or . . ."

"Or *what*?" Mom interrupted. "Tom will leave me?"

"Yes, he just might. He's at the end of his rope. He can't continue to go to work and handle everything here, too," Nina warned.

If anyone could get my mother to understand the seriousness of the situation, it was Nina. They had been friends for decades and now were sisters-in-law, having married brothers.

Mom started weeping while Nina comforted her. After a few minutes, she sent Mom off to get dressed.

"All right, now. Let's get this house in order," Aunt Nina commanded. In just a few hours, the dishes were washed, floors mopped, bed linens changed, and the mountains of laundry tackled.

And all I had to do was keep Ricky entertained. When my aunt was about to leave, I ran to her and whispered, "Thank you."

"Of course, my little Debbie. You call me if you need anything, anything at all," she whispered back.

Everyone still called me "Little Debbie" since I looked like the drawing of the girl on the box of Little Debbie snack cakes. It was getting annoying, though, since I was ten years old, almost eleven.

Today, I didn't mind.

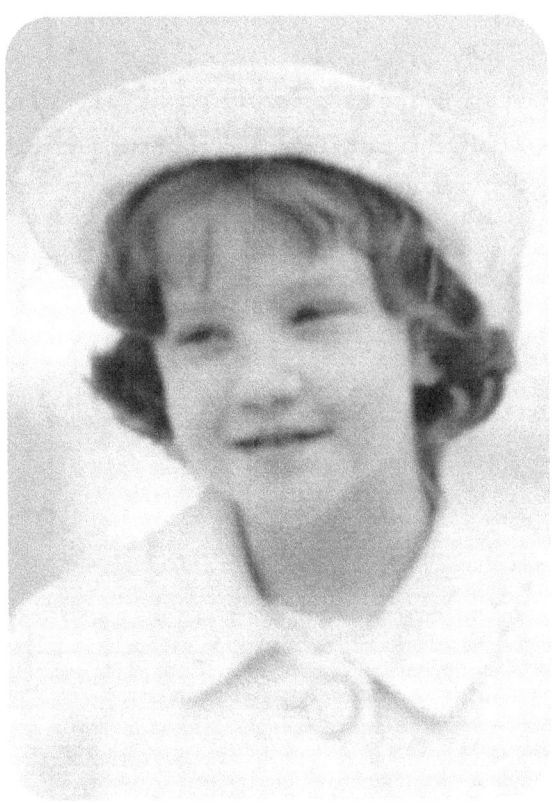

The summer months were worse since I didn't even have school to relieve me of caring for Ricky. Days were long, starting with getting Ricky's breakfast, and, depending on Mother's mood, I often had no time of my own the entire day.

If dishes were piled up in the sink and on the counter from the night before, I tackled them, hoping that would make Mom happy. And then, I would ask if I could swim in our above-ground pool that Daddy put up last summer. She usually would let me if Ricky was taking a nap.

I got the idea of teaching Ricky to swim so I could stay in the pool longer. Mom was comfortable if he was in his inner tube, but she got nervous when I started teaching him how to kick his legs and move his arms. He started progressing fast and soon could swim across the length of the pool. As Ricky improved, so did my confidence, and I felt bold enough to tell Mom, "Just go inside; I'm teaching Ricky how to swim."

Finally, she trusted me enough to allow us to swim all afternoon. Barb, my friend who lived on the corner, next to my grandparents' house, would come over and swim with us. We had completely different households. Both of her parents were morticians, and they lived above the funeral home they owned. Barb occasionally brought me into the viewing room; it was weird seeing dead people. But, after living in my crazy family, I had no idea what was normal.

I had a hard time deciding which Mother I preferred—the depressed, sullen one who stayed in her room and slept most of the day, or the obnoxious, flirty woman who pranced around in seductive outfits.

Neither version was a mother capable of raising children, especially one with special needs.

But maybe not everything was her fault, as she'd grown up in a poor, flawed family during the Depression. My mother was the youngest of four daughters born to Hulda and Alex Sutton, and the only one to graduate high school. My grandmother divorced Alex when her daughters were young; the rumor was that he was abusive, and she had to place her girls in a home for a while. Hulda then married Harry, a kind gentleman who was a decorated Purple Heart WW1 veteran. Grandpa Harry gave the family emotional security; however, their financial stability remained precarious. The four daughters were motivated to leave the house as early as possible. Shortly after graduating high school, my mother, the last girl to go, got a typing job for a few months, and then, she married Gordon Baarstad. She was just nineteen, had two children by age twenty-two, and divorced when she was thirty. She struggled with choosing alcoholic, abusive men who were attracted to her beauty and charm, not genuinely loving her for herself.

Until she met Tom Sughroue, her savior—he must have fallen hard for her, as he married her against his family's wishes, resulting in excommunication from his beloved Catholic religion. He married her despite the fact she had two teenagers, Rod and Cookie. Their marriage was difficult early on when I was born seven months later, bringing the number of mouths to feed to five. Tom was buying his father's farm in Irish Grove. All four Sughroue brothers farmed in the same county and helped each other harvest their crops. I was a toddler when the first tragedy struck. My father and Uncle Don were harvesting the corn crop, when the picker jammed, and Dad lost two fingers on his right hand.

My parents were forced to sell the farm to pay the medical bills, and we moved to the town of Pecatonica, where we lived in a small apartment above a tavern until I was five. It was cramped, with only two bedrooms. I shared a bedroom with my half-sister, Cookie. Her real name was Darlene, but she had acquired the nickname after the comic strip, *The Bumsteads*. Cookie baby-sat me when Mom worked at Mary Lester's fabric store. Rod, Mom's son, slept on the couch in the living room. He didn't seem to mind since he was busy in high school, playing basketball and dating his girlfriend, Nancy. From some conversations

I overheard, Rod and Cookie didn't have a very stable life until Mom married my father. I loved Nancy; she would spend time with me coloring pictures; one Easter, she helped me dye eggs. Sometimes, Rod and she would take me to the Seward Forest Preserve for a picnic.

Dad did several odd jobs to support our family, including selling door-to-door encyclopedias. When Cookie abruptly moved out to marry her boyfriend, I was sad. I remember many quarrels leading up to her departure; then, she was just gone one day, and Mom never talked about her again. Rod, Mom's son, joined the Navy and didn't visit often.

When there were just the three of us, I thought everything was perfect until my brother was born. From the time my parents brought Ricky home, something seemed off. At age seven, I knew our family had gone through lots of bad stuff: Dad's accident, losing the farm, and Cookie running away. Even a kid can detect tension, sadness, and stress. Mom seldom smiled anymore.

After Dad secured a manager's job at a home-decorating store, we could finally move out of the small apartment into a house. I didn't mind living on Main Street because I could visit "Sam's," the Five & Dime General Store, every afternoon after kindergarten. I loved Sam, the owner, an elderly man with a handlebar mustache who was always smoking a cigar. When I opened the store door, the bell would ring, and Sam would shuffle out from the back. "Ahh, there's my Little Debbie, my favorite customer." He would let me pick out a penny candy. After we moved to the house, I missed Sam and his candy gift, but having a yard to play in and a sidewalk to roller skate on made up for it.

The best part was that my grandparents' house was just one yard over if I cut across the neighbor's backyard. But Iola was a cranky older woman who didn't like anyone walking on her grass. I would dash across the back to Grandma's house if Iola was in her front yard, weeding her flowers. It was my one form of being naughty when I believed I needed to be perfect. I tried to visit my grandparents every day; Grandma had a weekly schedule of chores, and she would do a different one each day. Monday was laundry; she mopped floors on Tuesday, and so forth. But she always found time to bake daily—cookies, pies, cakes, strudel desserts, nut breads, and rolls. Grandma won several blue ribbons at the county fair each summer.

I loved playing cards with Grandpa; he finally taught me actual games after I fell for the "52-Card Pick-Up" gag.

"Debbie, want to play a new game?" he asked me one afternoon.

"Sure, Grandpa. "What's it called?"

"52-Card Pick-Up," he said, throwing all the cards on the floor. "You get to pick them up." He started laughing.

"Very funny," I said, while picking up the cards. I was slightly annoyed but could never be upset with him for long.

Being at their house gave me predictable order, love, and attention from the disorganized mess at my house and the unpredictable moods of my mother.

We had the best backyard, and my daddy was the most popular father in the neighborhood.

He truly was my hero.

"A father is the one friend upon whom we can always rely."
—Emile Gaboriau

Chapter Two

The Girl in the Black Raincoat
1964-1969, Illinois

From 1964 to 1968, I learned how to function in a dysfunctional family with help from my father, grandparents, Aunt Nina, and school friends. The most important lesson—unconditional love—I learned from my brother.

Mom had her "good" days, especially after she started working at the clinic, cleaning exam rooms every Wednesday. Doctor McGlothin had given my parents hope about their disabled son, and Mom became friends with Sandy, the receptionist, and Millie, the nurse. She was happier on those days and had more patience with Ricky.

Wednesday became one of my favorite days. Ricky stayed with my grandparents while I was at school, and I walked to their house with Barb, who lived next door.

The delicious smells of ginger and cinnamon met us as we walked through the front door of my grandma's house. We quickly dropped our school bags and sat down at the kitchen table. While enjoying Grandma's yummy ginger cremes, Barb and I talked about our day and then played a game of Candyland with Ricky. The game was helping him learn his colors. Seeing my friend accept my brother and enjoy him endeared Barb to me. She had been coming over to swim last summer and was finally comfortable with him.

After Barb went home, I played cards with Grandpa, who was teaching me the game of Euchre, while Grandma made dinner for all of us. On Wednesdays, my parents, grandparents, Ricky, and I would sit together and share a meal. After dinner, the adults would play cards; Mom and Dad laughed and kidded each other; sometimes, they would even hug. I sat next to Grandpa as he whispered his strategy secrets only to me. I felt safe and happy on those evenings.

My grandparents were devout Catholics and were very dismayed that I hadn't been baptized as an infant. The conservative priest had refused, arguing that I was the product of my parents' "sin" since they hadn't received the Sacrament of Matrimony because my mother was a divorcee. When a younger, more progressive priest came to town, Grandma convinced him to baptize Ricky and me. There were two other infants, along with my baby brother and seven-year-old me at the ceremony. I figured that maybe my dad forgot to get me baptized when I was a baby because he was so busy on the farm. Aunt Nina and Uncle Jerry were Ricky's godparents, and Rod's girlfriend, Nancy, was my godmother. It wasn't clear to me why my grandparents were so overjoyed and relieved, but if they were happy, so was I. After being baptized, I attended Saturday Catechism, learning that the Catholic Church was the *only* Church. I felt very proud and special but worried about my friends who went to the other churches in town, believing what the nuns taught us—that there was one

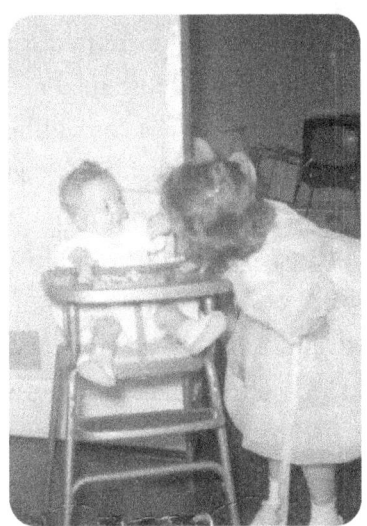

and only one true religion. Receiving my First Communion was momentous; I was the center of attention for once.

Sunday became my other special day with my father, as we would attend Mass, sitting in the last pew. I wondered if that was some rule, since Dad never received Communion. After Mass, we would go to the rectory, where Father Myers lived with his mother, and count the money envelopes from the collection basket. Enjoying Father Myers' mother's cinnamon rolls, we would sort the envelopes into two piles, one from the children, the other from the adults. Overseeing the children's donations made me feel extremely important, and Dad's total attention brought me great joy.

Mom and Ricky would usually be napping when we returned home; Daddy would say, "It's your turn to pick today's game." We'd play board games or cards, snacking on *Chicken in a Bisket* crackers and squirt cheese in a can.

Mom would say, "That's so disgusting." Daddy and I just giggled.

I never doubted my father's love, which compensated for my mother's indifference. His love and attention sustained me.

Ricky was thriving with all the "therapy" we were providing him at home, but Doctor McGlothin advised us that he needed time with children. After his admission to the Pecatonica Grade School Kindergarten class was denied due to his disability, my parents sought help from a private Catholic preschool in Rockford, Illinois. Dad could drive him on his way to work, as his home-decorating store was in the same city. The nuns embraced my brother without prejudice, and the children accepted him as well; although he was older, he was the same size they were.

Being around children helped improve Ricky's speech, and he developed social skills. Since Ricky was going to school, the pressure was off me having to work with him as often, allowing me to concentrate on my studies.

I graduated eighth grade with honors and completed my freshman year of high school. By spending more time at my friend's houses, I noticed how typical families functioned where there weren't dirty dishes all over the counter and baskets of unfolded laundry everywhere. I never understood why my mother was the way she was. She could seem normal one day—and bizarre and out of control the next. And she was always on the outs with someone; usually, it was one of her three sisters; Mom said they always betrayed her. Mom's family was very different from my father's. Grandma Hulda and Grandpa Harry never stayed in the same apartment for more than a couple of years, even though they all were in the same vicinity, similar in size, and above a business or store in downtown Rockford. It never made sense why they moved so frequently, until I overheard Grandpa ask Dad for rent money. They were either evicted for not paying their rent or moved to skip out of paying. Mom and Grandma argued quite often about her sisters. No one seemed happy or showed any affection. I wondered why we bothered to visit such misery.

I was much more comfortable visiting my dad's parents, which I did almost every day. Even though I was shy around all the aunts, uncles, and cousins when they came for Sunday dinner after Mass, there was laughter, fun, and plenty of hugs.

In June of 1969, our town of Pecatonica, population 1800, was planning for its Centennial Celebration. It was going to be an epic event with a weeklong carnival, culminating in a ball, with the participants wearing historic costumes. My mother worked on her 1800s-era ball gown for weeks; I never saw her so engaged or excited. On June 14, the final day of the celebration, I walked home with Jody after band practice. The Pecatonica High School Band was going to perform before the ball. Jody and I were excited because we were going to the carnival after the concert while our parents attended the ball, and Ricky was spending the night at my grandparents'.

After I arrived home, I started looking through piles of laundry for a white blouse and black slacks, which were the required concert attire. I was irritated with Mom. I'd reminded her that morning what I needed. *Could she ever do anything for me?* She seemed anxious and uneasy, already dressed in her exquisite ball gown; I had to admit she was very beautiful. Her natural red hair, enhanced by a monthly salon visit, accentuated her porcelain skin and emerald-green eyes. I just wished she would spend as much time on the household chores and my needs as she had on her makeup and hair.

"I wish your father would get home; he's always late," she complained.

"He probably had a late customer."

Dad had just started his own home-decorating business and was working hard to make it successful. But he had promised to leave the store early despite it being a Saturday, his busiest day, to see my band concert. In recent months, they had been quarreling often about how much time Dad was spending at his store. He was very excited about his business, and it was obvious that it made him happy. But Mother was selfish and demanding. In secret, I always supported my father and was on his side.

Hearing a car drive into our driveway, I announced, "That's probably Dad now." I looked out the window, only to see Sandy, the receptionist from the clinic, and her husband, Ken.

"It's Sandy and Ken,"

I looked back at Mom, confused at her reaction; she was white as a ghost and kept muttering, "No, no."

I had forgotten that Ken was the local coroner and the town's funeral director. In a small town, people wore many hats, despite blatant conflicts of interest.

I let them into the house; their faces were grim. They ignored me, going straight to Mom.

"Tom has been in an accident," Ken said quietly.

My mother screamed, falling to the floor, as Sandy went to her side. I didn't understand what was happening.

"What hospital is he at?" I yelled above my mother's crying. "Let's go."

"Your father is gone," Ken said, rather coldly.

"No!" I screamed back and began hitting his chest with my fists. "We need to go to the hospital."

"I'm sorry, Debbie. Your father was killed today in a car accident. We need you to be strong for your mother."

I ran upstairs to my room, slammed the door, and threw myself on my bed, sobbing uncontrollably. *It can't be true. It just can't be. How can I survive without my rock? Why couldn't it have been her?* I didn't open the door until my cousin JoAnn, Aunt Nina's daughter, knocked.

The next few days were a blur, as I shuffled numbly through the chaotic details of an unexpected, tragic death and tried to live up to everyone's expectations. At fifteen, I needed to be the "strong" one, the adult in the room, responsible for my mother's and brother's well-being. Of course, who wouldn't feel sorry for the grieving widow, now the single parent of a teenager and a Down-syndrome child? No one seemed to acknowledge the fact that I was also grieving the loss of a father, my only protector. All I heard was, "You need to be strong for your mother. It's up to you now."

Father Myers came to visit, offering his condolences. He tried to explain why my father, who went to Mass every Sunday and volunteered for many Church events, couldn't have a Catholic funeral Mass or be buried in the Catholic cemetery. My mother didn't seem to care, but I was horrified.

"What do you mean?" I asked.

"Well, your father was excommunicated from the Church when he married your mother."

"So, you're telling me that my father, who was a devout Catholic, who raised me to be the same, made sure I received all the Sacraments and attended Mass every Sunday, isn't good enough to have a funeral Mass or be buried in the sacred cemetery?"

"I'm sorry, Debbie. Your father was a good man."

"Oh, just not a good-enough Catholic?" I yelled at him.

I couldn't ignore the hypocrisy. Being a teenager who'd depended on the Church's foundation for stability, I felt abandoned again. First, my father had left me, and now I couldn't trust my religious beliefs. The "normal" parts of my life that had given me any sense of security were gone.

At the funeral home, I stood in silence, while the stream of people trailed in, one by one, offering their sympathies. The line was blocks long, taking hours to reach my mourning family, next to the open casket. Father Myers gave a sermon, which seemed futile to me. I glared at him while he spoke. I thought the entire debacle was obscene and unnecessary. It didn't change or help anything.

After the funeral, I asked my grandfather, "Why is life so unfair?"

"Oh, my little Debbie, life is like playing a game of cards. You may not always like the cards you're dealt, but you must play them to the best of your ability."

"What if I don't want to play anymore?"

"Life seems hard right now, but you're very strong," he told me as he held me close. "You know what your father would expect of you."

I kept my feelings of despair and helplessness to myself.

At first, there were people at the house all the time, bringing casseroles and cakes, more than we needed, and some of the Church ladies worked hard to get the house in order. After a couple of weeks, they needed to return to their own lives, and the three of us were left to pick up the pieces and move on.

Mom returned to taking naps during the day, wrapped in Dad's bathrobe and with a half-empty bottle on her nightstand; I was responsible for ensuring that Ricky was fed, bathed, and clothed. Since it was summer and I didn't have school, my life wasn't a priority. I'm unsure if it ever had been, at least to my mother.

No one noticed my depression, as I grew less interested in leaving the house. I began writing poetry to express my grief. I wasn't comfortable sharing these feelings with anyone. One poem, written in my journal that year, sums up how I was feeling.

I didn't think life could get worse. Until it did.

The Girl in the Black Raincoat

Mourners huddle together.
Beneath a canopy of canvas,
Protected from a summer shower.

Dearly Beloved. . . .
The words drown out soft sobbing.
Carefully folded American flag presented to the widow.
She clutches it to her chest as the
Little boy next to her whispers, "Where's Daddy?"

The Girl in the Black Raincoat

Twenty-one-Gun Salute startles; a baby cries.
Moment of silence.
A bugler plays "Taps, Day Is Done"
The crowd disperses, relieved to leave the sadness.

She stands alone.
The girl in the black raincoat.
Looking down into the deep, dark space.
Wanting to fall in, be with him, stay with him.
Her soul parent,
The one who understood and loved her.
She needed him.
Now, the weak one would need her more.

"We don't even know how strong we are until we are forced to bring that hidden strength forward."

—Isabel Allende

29

Chapter Three

❤

Betrayal

1969, Illinois

My cousin JoAnn and I were close friends growing up. She was a year older than me and more confident. I was shy and uneasy around people, even my relatives.

The Sughroues were a large extended family. Grandpa John and Grandma Emma had eight children, four boys and four girls. Four of these had their own large families of five or more children, so I had many cousins. But I never felt comfortable around any of them at Grandma's dinners after Sunday Mass or at the yearly family reunions.

Not that they weren't nice to me. But over the years, I had listened to my mother complain about them, telling me they were judgmental and hypocritical. She felt their disapproval because they blamed her for Dad's excommunication from the Catholic Church.

I inherited my mother's feeling of unworthiness and lack of acceptance. But being with JoAnn was different. Our families were extremely close, since her mom and mine had married brothers after being friends for decades. JoAnn helped me overcome my shyness at get-togethers, and I eventually realized my mother was wrong about my several aunts, uncles, and cousins. As I got older, I learned she had great contempt for other people. It was a sad way to live, and it was hard not to have contempt for her. It was starting to make sense—my mother may have been the reason Cookie ran away and Rod seldom called or visited.

Because I was embarrassed by my messy house and worried about kids making fun of my brother, I rarely invited schoolmates to my house for play dates, except for a couple of kids from the neighborhood; even then, we would play outside. Having JoAnn as my cousin and best friend was enough.

But things changed when JoAnn started high school. Since she had lost her baby fat, she liked showing off her thin figure by wearing short miniskirts and tight sweaters. She became rebellious and started hanging with "the wrong crowd." I heard Aunt Nina telling Mom that she was worried about her.

"She's becoming a wild child and totally out of control," Aunt Nina complained.

"We've tried grounding her and taking away privileges. But nothing works. Now she's dating a senior and coming home after her curfew."

When JoAnn became pregnant at the end of March 1969, everything got worse. She was forced to quit high school and wanted to marry the older boy. Despite their disappointments and concerns, Aunt Nina and Uncle Jerome gave their permission for the young couple to get married at the courthouse, and purchased a mobile home for them, placing it on their two-acre property. But there's a difference between "approval" and "blessing," and the tension between JoAnn and her parents was palpable.

It was a massive scandal for the conservative Catholic Sughroue family, and my grandparents were quite upset and ashamed. They felt JoAnn should have been sent away to an unwed-mothers home and given the baby up for adoption. At least then, she could have finished high school and have a future. But JoAnn's parents had no control over their daughter and eventually gave up trying to influence her decisions.

It seemed that's all the family talked about for months. One night, I overheard Mom and Dad discussing what should happen with the dilemma.

I interrupted and asked, "What would you do if *I* got pregnant?"

The look on my father's face told me the answer. He sternly replied, "No daughter of mine would be in that situation."

He had never sounded that cross with me before. It was very unsettling. I wasn't sure how to respond, so I retreated to my bedroom.

After Ken and Sandy announced my father's fatal car accident that summer day in June, I fled to my room, locked the door, and didn't answer until JoAnn pleaded with me to let her in. She crawled into my bed and held me until morning. JoAnn was more like a sister than a cousin.

We'd grown up together, spending most weekends with our parents, playing cards; we were inseparable, going together to Wisconsin for summer vacations.

But since her pregnancy and marriage, we'd drifted apart. Having her there to comfort me on that horrible day made it seem like we were still close, and it felt good having her back.

JoAnn and her husband, Ron, were offered a managerial position at Stuckey's, a gas station and convenience store on Route

20. Besides the salary, the job included free living quarters in the back of the store. The opportunity allowed them to move out of the trailer, and gave them independence and privacy.

JoAnn knew that the first Thanksgiving without my father was going to be difficult. She invited us to her new apartment for dinner with her parents, my aunt and my uncle. Her apartment was small, but it must have felt massive compared to the mobile home they'd been living in. It had an adequate-sized kitchen with an eating area large enough to accommodate the antique oak dining table Aunt Nina had gifted the newlyweds. They also had a second bedroom for a nursery, a good-sized living room, and a bath-and-a-half. Just like her mom, JoAnn kept her home clean and tidy.

She served the traditional Thanksgiving fare—turkey and stuffing, mashed potatoes and gravy, cranberries and pumpkin pie. But this holiday was far from typical. Everyone's grief over losing my father was still fresh and raw. Uncle Jerome missed his closest brother terribly, and my mother barely functioned most days.

Aunt Nina was feeling another loss: her daughter's future. Clearly, she wasn't looking forward to her grandchild's arrival next month. The sadness and tension were as thick as dense fog, the kind where you can't see two feet in front of you.

We ate silently; attempts at small talk were unsuccessful. It felt like there were fleeting thoughts floating in the air.

After dinner, I helped JoAnn clear the table and wash dishes. It was a relief to leave the adults' presence and be able to breathe.

"Why don't you spend the night?" my cousin asked. "We're having a few friends over, and it looks like you could use a break from your mom."

"Oh, I don't know."

I was still painfully shy around strangers and wondered if Rick would be okay alone with Mom.

JoAnn asked my mom, not waiting for my answer.

"Aunt Mavis, can Debbie spend the night? I could use her help."

"Uh, I guess." Mom said, looking at me for any reaction. I just shrugged my shoulders.

"Great—then it's settled. Thank you." JoAnn hugged my mom.

Shortly after the adults left, people started showing up with cases of beer and bottles of liquor. Mostly, they were Ron's male friends. This turn of events was making me feel uncomfortable.

Ron offered me a glass of whiskey, which I reluctantly accepted because I didn't want to appear like a prude. It burned my throat, and I wondered why anyone would want to drink such disgusting stuff. *Maybe it will help me forget my pain, even if for only a short time,* I thought.

After a couple more, I started feeling relaxed but dizzy and unsteady. My shyness was replaced with unmindful giddiness. I vaguely remember dancing and pushing someone away as they tried to kiss me. But when the nausea and lightheaded feeling overwhelmed me, I collapsed onto the couch. Then I blacked out.

When I came to and tried to sit up, I discovered that my pants were missing. I was wearing only panties—with the crotch ripped—and there was blood on the cushion underneath me. My groin area was sore.

Oh, my God, I thought.

It was clear that I had been raped. This horrific realization made me feel mortified and ashamed. At fifteen, I had only once ever kissed a boy. I tried to remember what had happened and who could have done this awful thing to me, and why, but my memory was fuzzy. Amid my drunken haze, before I passed out, I remembered moments of feeling pressure and heaviness.

I've disgraced my father.

I looked for my cousin, but she was still sleeping.

Does she know what happened last night? I wondered. *Why didn't she protect me?*

Her husband, Ron, was in the kitchen. He looked at me slyly and tried to hug me.

"Do not touch me. I need to go home."

He drove me back to my house in silence, and I was relieved that Mom and Ricky weren't home. I ran upstairs to the bathroom, eager to wash off my shame.

I filled the clawfoot tub with soapy water and soaked in the warmth; I felt utterly broken, without any desire to live. The abandonment and betrayal I experienced from people I depended on—my father, mother, and now my trusted cousin—felt like they would destroy me.

I picked up the razor from the soap dish, removed the blade, and, with a shaky hand, slowly brought it to my wrist.

Suddenly, I heard someone barreling up the stairs.

"Dabby, Dabby, where are you?" Ricky yelled. "Will you pway wif me?"

I dropped the blade.

What was I thinking? How could I be so selfish? What would happen to Ricky? Surely, he'd end up in an institution if I weren't here to take care of him.

I couldn't pass or fold my cards now. I just wished I'd finally get dealt a better hand.

Betrayal

"I'm coming, Sweetie." I quickly got out of the tub, dried myself off, and got dressed. I decided I must go on.

My brother had saved my life. And I kept the shameful secret to myself. Writing in my journal became my life preserver, as I was drowning in despair.

Trust

Trust n. confidence or faith in a person or thing
     v. to believe; to expect; to depend on

The meaning is simple
Yet ever so fragile
Destroyed in a moment

Innocence lost forever
Betrayal beyond belief
Trust replaced with shame

Broken spirit, barely alive
All alone in despair
Trust in self to survive

"Each betrayal begins with trust."

—Martin Luther

Chapter Four

❤

Happy Birthday?

1970, Illinois

After I stopped attending Catechism class on Saturdays and Mass on Sundays, Father Myers visited me at home—three times—in an attempt to bring me back into the fold.

When I asked him about his blind faith, he answered with ambiguity, causing more confusion and doubt in my adolescent mind. I couldn't tell if he was frustrated by my refusal to accept the Catholic teachings after the Church had rejected my father. Indeed, Father Myers had continued to show me patience and compassion.

I do know that Father Myers was deeply affected by my father's tragic death and the Church's denial of Catholic services. When I later heard he eventually left the priesthood, I wondered if my family's tragedy had led to his own disillusionment.

The following September, my sophomore year, I was still dealing with the grief of losing my father while trying to move on from the Thanksgiving incident, I met a new girl who'd just moved into town. Her bubbly personality drew me to her, and, despite my sullen demeanor, she took me under her wing.

Lisa invited me to her home, a large two-story house built on a hill, towering over a beautiful valley. I thought it was a mansion and believed her family must be wealthy. But her father, Jim, was a hardworking sales manager for the McKee Food Corporation, the company that made the snack cakes I was nicknamed after. They were just an average, middle-class family. Her parents immediately embraced and welcomed me into the family, quickly adopting my old, familiar nickname, "Little Debbie." Even though I hoped I had outgrown this past identity, hearing Lisa's dad saying it was comforting.

Lisa's mom, Gaye, was a traditional stay-at-home mother, her priority being her children. Unlike my mother, she kept a clean house, cooked wholesome meals, and was sincerely interested in her daughter's and son's lives. As Lisa's new best friend, I was also the lucky recipient of such care and interest. Observing their loving family interactions made me want something different for myself.

Becoming aware of how "normal" families functioned, combined with my emerging adolescent rebellion, I became more defiant to my mother's increasing demands. Ricky was still my priority; my mother's approval was at the bottom of my list of goals. As my self-esteem grew, so did Mom's dependence and erratic behavior. When she realized I was no longer the dutiful daughter she could control, her drinking increased to a level that was unsafe for all of us. Often, she was at the tavern when I came home from school, leaving Ricky with a neighbor and the cupboards and refrigerator mostly empty.

During one of our screaming matches, Mom demanded that I show her more respect. I replied, "When you start behaving like a mother, I'll give you respect."

I had finally found my voice. There was no turning back.

The more time I spent at Lisa's house, the less tolerance I had for my own unkempt home. I didn't want to live like this any longer.

I reached out for help by calling my half-brother Rod. We barely knew each other; he'd joined the Navy after graduating high school in 1958, when I was four. He never returned home until my father's funeral. After the service, Rod took me aside and asked, "How are you doing?"

"Why do you care?" I replied sarcastically. "I haven't seen you for years."

"I know, Debbie. I'm sorry for that. It's just busy with the kids."

Rod was a successful court reporter, living in Chicago with his wife, Donna, and their three sons. The last time I'd seen him was at his wedding, when Ricky was a baby. My mother never approved of Rod's wife, which strained their relationship even more.

"Your dad was a good man. I had a great deal of respect for him. And I know how difficult Mother can be, which is why I've not visited more. But, if you need anything, please call." He slipped his business card into my hand. He stayed a few extra days, trying to settle my family's finances, which weren't good, due to my father's new, struggling business.

Memorial Day was coming up, which happened to be my sixteenth birthday. I hoped I could use the holiday weekend as a reason to get away for a few days. Rod agreed to come get me that Friday and bring me back home on Monday to celebrate my birthday with Mom and Ricky. He promised to address her drinking, her total dependence on me for Ricky's care, and her apparent disdain for common household responsibilities.

I had a relaxing weekend playing with Rod's three boys, Roddy Jr., Andy, and Christopher. They seemed to have a happy, typical family. I quickly noticed what a loving, attentive mom Donna was. And she seemed genuinely concerned about my welfare. I realized that my mother had lied about Donna; she was a kind, unselfish person.

On the drive back to my house, I tried not to worry about the impending confrontation with my mother and trusted that my half-brother would be able to get through to her. The feeling of dread quickly returned as we pulled into the driveway, and I saw Ricky sitting in the middle of it. His clothes were filthy, and his dirty, tear-stained face said a lot about how his weekend without me had gone. He ran to me and began sobbing when I picked him up.

What have I done? I thought. *I should have never left him.*

Seething with rage, I went into the house, screaming for my mother. I bounded up the stairs to her bedroom, where she was barely awake. I didn't hold back: every horrible thought came out of my mouth. I told her I was done and threatened to take Ricky away; she didn't deserve us. And then I went back downstairs to my brother's family.

Suddenly, Mother stumbled down the stairs, looking deranged, with a crazed look. She went into the kitchen, grabbed a butcher knife out of the drawer, and sliced her forearm. Rod managed to catch her and quickly wrapped a kitchen towel around the blood-spurting wound. It was chaos. Ricky and my nephews were shrieking; Rod was shouting orders to call Ken and Dr. McGlothin and yelling at Donna to take the boys outside. I just stood there in shock, not able to move or speak.

It was all my fault.

Dr. McGlothin put a few stitches in the cut, added a compression bandage, and Ken (aka the coroner, funeral director, and ambulance driver) drove us to the hospital. My mother was stabilized in the ER and then transferred to Singer Mental Hospital because she had attempted suicide. Rod had called Aunt Nina and asked her to go to the house to clean up the blood before we returned. No one had any energy to talk. I was sure everyone blamed me. After all, my hurtful words had led my mother to do this.

Rod and his family left for Chicago, and as I watched them drive away, I had an envious thought: Rod left when he was 18 and was leaving again. I wondered if I would *ever* be able to leave. His parting words failed to comfort me. "Hang in there, kid," he said before he left. "Call if you need anything." I was certain he hoped I wouldn't.

I returned to the house and started packing for our stay at Aunt Nina's. Noticing the tears welling up in my eyes, she walked over and hugged me.

"Don't worry, Little Debbie. Maybe now your mother can finally get the help she needs."

She looked around the messy kitchen.

"I'm so sorry we didn't realize how serious your living situation was."

I thought her words were insincere. She knew. Rod knew. All the adults in my life were aware. I tried not to begrudge them. They had their own lives, and they did show up for the crisis moments. I realized that it was up to me to figure out this mess.

"Oh, I almost forgot," Aunt Nina said. "Happy Birthday."

This was one birthday better left forgotten.

The next day, Grandma and Grandpa came to wish me a happy birthday. Grandpa pulled a small package from his pocket and said, "I thought you could use this."

It was a brand-new deck of playing cards.

He placed the deck in my hands, held them with his, and said, "I want you to promise me something, my granddaughter. Never stop playing. You're sad and angry right now. But nothing is either all bad or all good. Look for the positives to be grateful for, and find joy in simple things. Then, my dear, you won't be sad forever."

"I won't, Grandpa. I promise."

I wanted to believe him, but some days, I could barely get out of bed. If not for believing Ricky was completely dependent on me, I may have given up entirely.

My English teacher had given me the book *The Prophet*, by Kahlil Gibran. Some of it didn't make sense to me, but I picked it up one day after visiting Mom at the hospital. The chapter "Joy and Sorrow" spoke to me.

"The deeper that sorrow carves into your being, the more joy you can contain.

"When you are joyous, look deep into your hearts, and you shall find it is only that which has given you sorrow that is giving you joy.

"When you are sorrowful, look again in your heart, and you shall see that in truth you are weeping for that which has been your delight."

It was true that I had experienced not only deep sorrow but also intense joy, being Ricky's sister.

My other favorite quote of Kahlil that helped me was, "Your living is determined not so much by what life brings to you as by the attitude you bring to life; not so much by what happens to you as by the way your mind looks at what happens."

I finally understood what Grandpa had been trying to teach me: I couldn't control everything; I couldn't choose my "cards" or control others' behavior. I couldn't change the past, but I could decide how to react to negative things in my life. I was in charge of my attitude, thoughts, and actions. I could choose strength or weakness, bitterness or love, despair or hope, anger or forgiveness.

One thing I knew for sure: I didn't want to become my mother.

"I am not what happened to me. I am what I choose to become."
—Carl Jung

Chapter Five

A New Perspective and a Time for Healing

1970, Illinois

Family counseling became a mandatory part of Mom's treatment plan after her suicide attempt. She was being treated for severe depression with manic episodes, triggered by the birth of a developmentally disabled son and further exacerbated by the sudden death of her husband.

After Mom's mood swings were stabilized with medication, she was able to manipulate the therapists with her charming wit. She quickly convinced them that nothing was her fault; her drastic actions were due to her circumstances: she was a grieving widow left to take care of a disabled son and rebellious teenage daughter.

My silent defiance in response to the therapists' questions confirmed their diagnosis, and my mother was discharged after three weeks. Just as my faith in the Catholic religion had diminished, so did my trust in adults. I was certain that the therapists were not interested in my side of the story, given my age and Mother's believable charisma.

I did like one therapist, though; she had given me a book, *On Death and Dying*, by Elisabeth Kübler-Ross, describing the five stages of grief. After reading the book, I realized I had been stuck in the anger stage for a long time. It was time to move on, but how?

I read another book that summer: *Are You There, God? It's Me, Margaret*, a novel by Judy Blume. Even though I stopped attending Mass, I hoped to—no, I *needed* to—believe in God or some higher power. I liked how, in the book, Margaret talked to God, asking questions as if speaking to a friend.

I had already been talking to my father during my daily walks on the prairie path in the back of our house, which used to be railroad tracks. Instead of reciting childhood prayers that

now held no meaning, I began to ask God about my doubts and concerns. Sometimes, answers would come to me during a dream, or an idea would pop into my mind as I awakened. It was weird and reassuring at the same time.

Remembering the advice Grandpa had given me when he brought me the deck of cards for my birthday, I tried to find the positives in my life, specifically about my mother. She was an excellent seamstress, had raw artistic talent, and was extremely creative. The things Mom accomplished during her manic episodes were incredible, such as an impressive oil-painting portrait of my great-grandmother that looked like it had been painted by a professional.

Before Ricky was born, Mom had been my second-grade room-mother and would stay up all night creating complex party favors for school parties. Her sewing skills were flawless, and she was commissioned to sew the high-school cheerleader outfits one year. Our living-room window holiday displays were as elaborate as Macy's in downtown Chicago. She was stunningly beautiful, and her charming personality drew people to her, especially those unaware of her dark side. I understood why my father loved her.

But without having developed any coping skills from her own dysfunctional childhood, and because of the generational alcohol abuse she'd endured, Ricky's diagnosis began Mom's downward spiral. The sudden death of her husband completed the collapse.

Perhaps my assumption that she didn't love me was wrong. As I tried to imagine how she was feeling and how things looked from her perspective, an amazing revelation occurred to me. I developed a sense of empathy, and my anger diminished.

At the beginning of July, I tried a new approach and asked her for help.

"Mom, could you teach me how to sew? I would love some new clothes for school, and I know we can't afford store-bought things."

"Really?" Mom asked. Her eyes lit up as she rushed to her hoarding closet and came out with bolts of fabric she'd accumulated from working at the Mary Lester fabric store. The last time I'd seen her this excited was when she'd made her Centennial-era ball gown.

I had no idea she had this much fabric, sewing patterns, and notions. Not only could she sew, but she also had a distinctive fashion flair. In the following weeks, we worked together, constructing my new school wardrobe, while developing an *actual* mother-daughter relationship. She asked about my new friend, Lisa, and seemed genuinely interested in my life for the first time in years.

"Let's invite Lisa for lunch; I'd love to meet her."

I had no idea how to respond. This could go horribly wrong, exposing my secret home life to a friend. But I didn't want to curtail Mom's newfound enthusiasm.

"Okay," I reluctantly replied. I knew I had to give my mother a chance since she was making real progress for the first time since Dad had died.

I made the living room presentable, while Mom cooked a delicious lunch of homemade macaroni and cheese, a fresh green salad, and apple crisp for dessert. My mother was also known for her culinary skills—just not housework.

The lunch visit went well. Mother was on her best sober behavior, charming Lisa with her quick wit and dry sense of humor. Ricky was as adorable as ever.

After lunch, I took Lisa to the prairie path, sharing my peaceful, serene place with my best friend, since I had already divulged my nontypical family.

"You are so lucky," Lisa exclaimed.

"You've got to be kidding me," I responded, rolling my eyes.

"I mean . . . uh, I feel bad that you lost your dad—and about your brother's disability. But your mom is so cool. And Ricky is a doll."

This was unbelievable. The girl who lived in the massive house on the hill, had an overflowing closet of the latest fashion trends, owned her own car, and had two doting parents and a normal brother—was jealous of me. Me—who lived in a broken-down, unkempt house with an unpredictable, mentally ill mother, no father, and a brother who required everything.

"My parents drive me crazy," she explained. "They're so controlling and strict, I can't even breathe. They don't trust me to make my own decisions; sometimes, I can't stand them. Your mom lets you be you."

"Since Rick was born, I've had to stand up to people who were picking on me and making fun of my brother. You have no idea how hard it is,"

"Exactly," Lisa said. "You aren't afraid to stand up or speak out."

"And you are? Why?"

"Because I care too much about what people think of me. I'm not strong—I don't have your courage. Well, I better get going, or my mom will have a hissy fit. Thank your mom for lunch. This was fun."

I went back inside the house; Mom and Ricky were snuggling on the couch, watching cartoons. It had been a good day for them, too.

I retreated to my room, sat in my favorite place by the window, looked out at our backyard, and thought about what had transpired today.

What an epiphany. Lisa's life appeared wonderful on the outside, but, inside, it was far from a perfect life. Even though her mental and physical spaces were filled with material things and smothering attention, she had *her* issues, too.

Maybe money and material things aren't that important. Maybe an easy life wasn't that beneficial in the long run. Maybe caring for others rewarded you more, I thought.

It was a matter of perspective. I could feel sorry for myself for what my life lacked or be grateful for the life lessons in survival.

I was needed and important to my brother and mother. That gave me confidence and a sense of identity. I discovered that my mother wanted to be needed and valued, too. Everyone needs to feel they're worthy.

Suddenly, I couldn't wait to start my junior year of high school with this new insight—and with a beautiful, unique wardrobe that couldn't be found in any store.

For the first time, I was starting to look forward to a new day without being so sad and angry.

"You have power over your own mind—not outside events. Realize this, and you will find strength."

—Marcus Aurelius

Chapter Six

The Game of Euchre, or the Game of Life?

1971, Illinois

G randpa taught me the basic rules of Euchre when I was eight; by the time I was ten, I understood his strategic style of play.

"Most people play it safe, only making trump when winning three tricks is more likely," he told me. "But there's no thrill in an easy win. The accomplishment comes when you take a chance and win the hand with strategy." All the lessons Grandpa taught me playing Euchre were beginning to carry over into my life. Grandpa explained why he hardly ever passed the chance to make trump: "Don't give your opponent the upper hand."

"But what if you don't think you can win the tricks?" I asked, unconvinced by his reasoning.

"That's where the strategy comes in. Understand your partner's style of play. Choose your partner carefully, one that complements your style. You don't have to be exactly alike but must respect each other's choices."

Was he talking about a card-game partner or a future-life partner? I wondered. Sometimes, it wasn't easy to tell if he was still talking about playing Euchre or conveying guidance for my life.

"Remember, if you lose one hand, it's not the entire game. What you learn about your opponent's play is crucial to the next hand. For example, if you lead trump, and they don't play any, you know your next play."

Grandpa might lose a hand or two, but he seldom lost the game. When we were partners, we hardly ever lost, because we knew exactly how the other played.

I would think about Grandpa's strategy lessons during my daily walks on the prairie path. Overcoming difficult issues without anger and bitterness was my new life goal. I strove not to compare my situation with anyone else's, and I felt pride in each accomplishment.

I started my junior year in high school with a new determination to succeed. Vowing to take risks, I applied for the photographer position on the yearbook staff, volunteered for the Junior Prom planning crew, and was nominated to be class vice-president. It was an exciting year, as my leadership skills evolved and my popularity grew. Grandpa was right: the more I ventured out of my comfort zone and succeeded, the more my confidence grew.

Playing it safe was no longer an option. I was in charge of my life, refusing to be a victim of circumstances. Instead, I'd be a creator of opportunities.

"The only person you are destined to become is the person you decide to be."

—Ralph Waldo Emerson

Chapter Seven

You're Not Alone—I've Got You

1970-1975, Illinois

I had met Jeff Miller, a senior, toward the end of my sophomore year in high school. He was different from the other boys I'd dated. Not that there were many, but they all seemed to want something from me. I was uncomfortable with them pawing at my chest and sticking their tongue in my mouth; I usually refused second dates. After the Thanksgiving assault, I stopped dating altogether.

We met on the bus going on a field trip to the Field Museum of Natural History in Chicago. By the time we reached our destination, it felt like I had known him for months. I agreed to a date the next weekend. When Jeff walked me to the front porch after our first date, he gave me a quick kiss on my cheek, squeezed my hand, and thanked me for a nice time. After that, we'd talk for hours, and he listened as I related the sorrow of losing my father. They'd met once when Dad went to Jeff's house to show his mother wallpaper samples, and Jeff had thought Dad was nice. Jeff even asked about Rick, and I felt comfortable sharing my concerns about his future welfare. His genuine interest and compassion for my well-being were apparent.

Jeff graduated in 1970 and enlisted in the Marine Corps; we kept in touch by writing letters. We hadn't declared an exclusive commitment to each other, but even so, I had lost interest in dating anyone else. My focus was on grades and going away to college.

Lisa and I started considering what university we wanted to attend. Of course, we planned to attend the same one and be roommates. A scholarship would pay my tuition, even at an expensive, smaller private school, which the school counselor recommended for me. However, Lisa preferred a larger state university, and I was determined to stay with her, even if it wasn't the best fit for me.

My senior year of high school was the best in terms of personal success and self-confidence. Even though I wasn't a cheerleader, I had been voted Homecoming Queen. It would have been a positive memorable event—if Mother hadn't shown up drunk.

I was still the yearbook photographer and enjoyed attending all the sports competitions, club meetings, and social activities, documenting high-school life through posed pictures. However, the more-candid photos I took, which caught the genuine, fleeting moments of student life, were my favorite and gave me the most pride and recognition. My work didn't go unnoticed, and I was recruited—along with Lisa—to be the senior yearbook editors. We worked hours after school for months and produced—according to our advisor, Miss Ottenhausen—the most unique, artistic high-school annual in years.

Ignoring my internal doubts, I agreed to attend Western Illinois University (WIU) in Macomb, Illinois, as Lisa's roommate. It was only a three-hour drive from Pecatonica, which would allow me to make frequent weekend home visits to relieve any homesickness.

It was a confusing and unsettling time for me; the popular, confident high-school senior was lost in a sea of contradictions. Despite years of hopeful anticipation, dreaming of leaving my family's dysfunction, I found myself insecure, unsure of my goals, and ill-equipped to deal with the unfamiliar stresses of college life. My grades suffered after I lost interest in my classes, as did my aspirations. My personal accountability was mixed up with my identity as my brother's caregiver and my mother's support system. I wasn't sure who I was or wanted to be.

When Lisa transferred to her boyfriend's small, private college after our first year, I felt abandoned again and regretted that I hadn't gone with my first choice, Marycrest College, the private women's school, instead of following my friend. Unfortunately, after the first semester of my sophomore year, I had no energy or interest in pursuing a transfer or remaining at WIU. College life had lost its appeal, and I only wanted to leave.

I went home for winter break in December 1973 and stayed. My mother's display of disappointment in my decision to drop out of college was suspect; I knew she was relieved to have me home. However, since I'd been gone for nearly two years, Mom and Rick had developed a routine: she worked as a waitress, and my brother attended a new special-education grade school in Winnebago, a small town a few miles away. It seemed my absence had benefited them. They now relied on each other and were doing better than I was.

Unfocused, with no direction, I wandered aimlessly from one idea to another. I considered the Peace Corps as well as enlisting in the armed forces. Army and Air Force recruiters would arrive at the house unannounced, responding to a no-postage-required information card I'd impulsively filled out and mailed.

In addition to Mom's day job as a waitress at the diner, she also cooked the Friday night fish fry at the local pub. Rick stayed with a neighbor, leaving me free to do whatever, which meant staying home reading. After a few weeks, I was no closer to a future game plan.

One Friday night, near the end of January, Mom called home.

"Deb, remember that boy, Jeff, you've been writing to? He's home on leave and at the bar, asking about you. Why don't you come up and have dinner?"

Jeff met me at the door and gave me a friendly hug.

"Why didn't you tell me you weren't returning to school?" he asked.

"Ashamed, I guess. I've never been a quitter, and now, I feel like a failure."

"You're not a failure. Stop being so hard on yourself. Look at what you accomplished in high school despite your family's struggles. Maybe you just need a break, a reset, some time to reevaluate your priorities. You're only 19."

His words filled my heart, and I felt less disappointed in myself. We went out a few times before his leave ended and grew closer. On the last night, he hugged me tight and said, "See you in August." His four-year tour of duty would be up, and he wasn't sure about re-enlisting.

"Not sure where I'll be in August," I replied.

"Hopefully, you'll wait for me to return before you make any decisions."

"I can't make any promises. Sorry,"

A WIU friend, Sue, contacted me unexpectedly at the end of February; she was planning to drop out after the semester ended and suggested we get an apartment together in the summer. We decided to meet in the next few months to determine where to live.

I had no prospect of employment to pay for future living expenses, but at least I had a plan, and the timeline provided an incentive. If I were going to live on my own, a job was imperative. After several interviews, I accepted a position at St. Vincent's Home for severely developmentally disabled children and teens. Even though I didn't have a degree, my life experience with my brother was deemed valuable by the administration. The facility, located in Freeport, Illinois, 30 minutes from my mother's home, was where Sue preferred to find an apartment. My starting date was September 3, after Labor Day, and Sue and I hoped to find a place in Freeport before the end of the month.

On August 1, I received a letter from Jeff with a surprising invitation. He wanted me to fly to Cherry Point, North Carolina, on his last day and proposed we drive to Florida and visit all the attractions, including Walt Disney World. It was a very tempting offer: an all-expenses-paid vacation plus an opportunity to fly for the first time. Despite my excitement, I had reservations and concerns about the sleeping arrangements. I was now 20 years old and still considered myself a virgin, since it wasn't my choice not to be. And I was not in any hurry for that kind of relationship.

"Since you're paying for this trip," I bluntly asked, "will you be expecting something in return, as in sleeping together?"

"Of course not," was his quick reply. "Debbie, you should know by now I sincerely respect you. After four years of serving my country, I deserve a vacation and want to spend time with you. We have a connection, don't we?"

Jeff calmed my fears about his motives, and I gratefully accepted his offer, flying to North Carolina on August 15. He had never given me any indication not to trust him.

We enjoyed two weeks together, first staying a few days with his Staff Sergeant Steve Glasgow's family at the North Carolina base. Watching Jeff interact with Steve's children revealed another side of him: He had a natural, relaxed manner around kids, suggesting he had potential as a good parent.

Was I falling in love? Or did I just desperately need normalcy, security, and to feel safe?

After leaving North Carolina, we headed south on I-75, sometimes talking and discovering new things about each other, other times driving silently. Either way, our days were enjoyable and relaxing. Our connection deepened after spending 24 hours a day together for two weeks. The nights were spent cuddling, with only light fondling and kissing, and no pressure from Jeff to go beyond my comfort level. I felt like a giddy teenager, accepting a huge Winnie the Pooh stuffed animal Jeff bought me at Walt Disney World. He laughed, watching me struggling to carry the life-size toy through the crowd. I loved that big bear and secretly imagined decorating a future baby nursery around it.

We arrived home in Illinois at the end of August, each returning to our individual lives. I started working at St. Vincent's and collecting items for Sue's and my new apartment. Jeff temporarily moved back to his parents' until he could find a job.

Sue and I moved into the Freeport apartment and adjusted to living as roommates. When I'd decided to live with her, I never anticipated the development of a close relationship between Jeff and me. I juggled Sue and Jeff's expectations for weeks while assessing my priorities.

Jeff and I had professed our love to one another, but marriage seemed a long way off. I was still coping with my childhood demons and not very confident in my judgment, as my trust and abandonment issues remained unresolved. I'd placed them in a pocket, to grapple with in the future. But on New Year's Eve, Jeff proposed.

"You do understand that I will most likely be responsible for my brother in the future," I said, testing him. "We are a package deal."

"Yes, I've considered that. I love you and your brother. And I care about your mother, too."

Not convinced, I replied, "You have no idea what you're signing up for."

"Maybe not, but I want to spend my life with you. If that means committing to your brother as well, then I do," he said, taking me into his arms.

"You don't have to go alone. I've got you."

"The best way to find out if you can trust somebody is to trust them."

—Ernest Hemingway

Chapter Eight

Wife, Mother, Coach

1975-1981, Illinois

It took me a month to answer Jeff's proposal; nevertheless, I reluctantly agreed to marry him.

I hesitated for many reasons: my age and inexperience, unresolved childhood trauma, abandonment, and trust issues. I worried that his desire to be my savior and my need for security could be problematic in the future. That didn't sound like the recipe for a successful, long-term marriage.

But my love for him outweighed my uncertainty, and we set a date for June 7, 1975, one week after my twenty-first birthday. Mom was thrilled to have a future son-in-law who would accommodate her requests for household projects.

I felt terrible about leaving Sue stuck with the apartment, but she quickly found another girl as a replacement roommate. I had done the abandoning for the first time, and it didn't feel good, as it damaged our relationship.

Even though Jeff was also a disenchanted Catholic, we made our families happy by agreeing to marry at St. Mary's, our childhood parish. Mother could have cared less, but my favorite grandma was still alive, as were all my aunts and uncles. Grandpa Sughroue had died the summer after I graduated high school, on the Fourth of July. Many holidays representing traumatic events in my life were beginning to add up and would trigger difficult feelings. My father was killed on Flag Day, a day before Father's Day. Thanksgiving became a day of not being thankful. My birthday represented my mother's suicide attempt, for which I still blamed myself. I probably should have considered therapy, but, instead, I pushed everything down in suppressed denial.

Our first meeting with Father Clausen was strained and uncomfortable for me. He told me I needed to name a "father" figure to walk me down the aisle to "give" me away when I told him I would be walking alone. Since the only respected and trusted men in my life—my father and grandfather—were gone, there wasn't anyone I wanted to escort me.

He glanced at Jeff and then at me, and said, "This is highly unorthodox and not recommended. You need to reconsider."

"I mean no disrespect, Father, but no one can take my father's place; I will walk alone. I don't need anyone to 'give' me away. I will walk down the aisle alone, or we will reconsider this parish," I replied adamantly.

"I see," Father Clausen answered. Looking at Jeff and winking, he said, "You will have your hands full with this one."

"I'm good, Sir," Jeff told him.

Mom was eager to help with the wedding and engaged her friends to assemble reception-hall decorating and food teams. Her creativity transformed the dull, dreary American Legion Hall, Post 197, into a colorful, festive reception venue. She led the food team in making a delicious and hearty Midwest

comfort-food menu. Despite our meager budget, both the wedding and reception turned out beautifully. The ceremony was a mix of a traditional Catholic Sacrament of Matrimony, complete with a Mass and untraditional elements. In addition to walking down the aisle solo, I didn't play the classic Wedding March but chose "The Wedding Song *(There Is Love)*" by Paul Stookey. At St. Vincent's School. I worked with a teacher musician who agreed to coordinate and have his band play the music for the ceremony, mostly '70s folk music. We were told later that the music was the best they had ever heard at a wedding, and that there wasn't a dry eye in the church.

Father Clausen was right: we were definitely unorthodox— some would call us "hippies." We spent our honeymoon camping in a tent.

Afterward, we settled into married life. While figuring out our roles, our first difference of opinion was unearthed, which was related to our different upbringings. Jeff was raised in a traditional family, where his father worked, and his mother stayed home, taking care of the household. I'd never seen his father helping with domestic chores other than taking out the garbage.

It didn't make sense to me that Jeff thought I'd come home from work to prepare dinner, wash dishes, do laundry, and clean the house.

The fact that the wife was expected to do two jobs didn't sit well with me, and I didn't hesitate to share this with my new husband. Fortunately, Jeff listened to my rationale and my thoughts on the ridiculous disparity in gender roles.

"Gosh, Deb. I never thought about it. That's just how my parents did things."

"Well, I'm here to tell you this is not what I signed up for. I will not work all day for you to come home and sit on the couch while I make dinner and take care of everything else."

"You're right," he said. "We both work; we should share the household chores."

Together, we worked on an equitable plan for sharing responsibilities. Whoever returned home first would start dinner, and we'd wash the dishes together. Cleaning our small apartment was quick work, which left us more free time.

Jeff's sisters were surprised at how much their brother helped me.

"What do you mean?" I asked. "He's not 'helping me.' We're both contributing to our daily living requirements. What's the big deal? I hear you complain all the time about your husbands doing nothing."

"Well, when Matt helps me," Patty said, "he doesn't do anything right or up to my standards."

"That's ludicrous. Do you want help or not? No wonder he stopped if all you do is criticize him."

It was apparent my idea of marriage was different from theirs. As they continued to gripe about their lives, I was happy in mine.

Jeff and I had resolved this first problem together, but our early married years would continue to be challenging. Six months after our wedding, I was pregnant with our first daughter. I gave birth to our second daughter, Jamie, when Kelly was 16 months old. In three short years, I'd become a wife and the mother of two babies less than two years old, and I was just 23.

Mom rose to the occasion, becoming my support system, reversing our previous roles, when she depended on me. She reveled in her role as grandmother and seemed pleased when I felt inadequate or apprehensive as a new mother. I wondered if she was compensating for her own parental failure by becoming a doting grandmother. She spent hours sewing and knitting the girls exquisite dresses, sweaters, and blankets; as they got older, she made them intricate clothes for their Barbie and Cabbage Patch dolls. I graciously accepted her help and gifts, ignoring the occasional barb she still felt the need to inflict. It seemed she felt empowered by criticizing me, uplifting her ego. Instead of positive encouragement and confidence-building praise, she sought to undermine my parenting at every stage. She disapproved of pacifiers and made fun of my homemade baby food made from vegetables out of our garden. I bit my tongue and remained silent because I needed her help. Now, I understood why Cookie had left, never to return, and wondered how long I could endure Mom's sick and unhealthy treatment of me. Her loving relationship with my daughters outweighed my discomfort and emotional pain. And, of course, Jeff was always supportive, which helped. I learned to choose my battles.

My brother accepted his title, "Uncle Ricky," with great pride; the adoration between my girls and him was apparent and equal. His patience never wavered as they climbed into his lap, asking for one more story. He would play with them for hours, building block castles, coloring masterpieces, or assembling puzzles.

This attentive care from Grandma and Uncle Ricky allowed me to tackle the mounting household chores: washing mounds of diapers, tending to the vegetable garden, and cleaning the house. As the girls got older, their care became more manageable. But Mom continued to undermine my parenting, preferring to sabotage any structure or limits I tried to enforce. She even would write absence excuses to the school administration when they were in high school.

A significant change occurred with special education in the late '70s. When Rick started high school in 1978, the new movement of mainstreaming disabled students with non-disabled students was being introduced at Winnebago High School. However, the program lacked direction or implementation. The Special Ed students were removed from the isolation of their previous school and placed in the regular high school. The premise that all students were entitled to equality in education was honorable in theory but had significant shortfalls. The consequence was that students didn't know how to behave with each other or how to express acceptance.

This lack of awareness and misunderstanding of the Special Ed students' disabilities or abilities led to brutal teasing and bullying from the other kids. The disabled students, who had been sheltered in Special Education classes, consequently lacked appropriate social interaction with typical teens.

Some of the disabled youngsters, including my brother, acted out in response. Mom received a call from the principal requesting a parent-teacher conference about Ricky's bad behavior. There was a complaint from a cheerleader's parent that Rick was bothering the girl by continuing to ask her to be his girlfriend. He'd also pushed the girl's boyfriend, telling him to leave Mary alone. The principal warned my mother that Rick could be suspended if his behavior continued.

"Debbie, what am I going to do?" Mom cried. "Will you go to the meeting? I can't listen to them complain about your brother. Please. I'll watch the girls."

"Of course, I'll go. But, Mom, this is serious. Ricky cannot behave like this."

"It's not his fault. Those kids are being mean to him. You should hear the names they call him."

I had exactly one week to prepare for the meeting with the principal, counselor, and Ricky's Special Education homeroom teacher. I went to the library to research the pros and cons of mainstreaming and inclusion, to try to understand why this approach was failing in Winnebago. After speaking to other parents, it became apparent that many of the disabled students felt left out and unaccepted by their typical peers.

When I'd worked at St. Vincent's before my daughters were born, I was introduced to Special Olympics, an organization whose mission is to bring all persons with intellectual disabilities into the larger society, where they're accepted, respected, and given a chance to become productive citizens. The organization is founded on the belief that people with intellectual disabilities can, with proper instruction and encouragement, learn, enjoy, and benefit from participation in individual and team sports.

I had an idea that the Special Olympics' vision of transforming communities might be considered as a solution to other mainstreaming issues. Perhaps it could inspire the non-disabled students to open their minds to accept and include people with disabilities—or anyone perceived as "different."

Before the school conference meeting, I carefully planned a presentation, introducing Special Olympics and focusing on the program's benefits.

First, I listened to the complaints about Rick's behavior, agreeing that some intervention was needed. However, I asked if a positive strategy could be considered instead of a negative punishment.

"Are other students acting out?" I asked. "Have you asked the disabled students why they have behaved in this manner?"

"Um, I'm not sure," the principal stammered. He looked at Miss Beckman, the Special Ed homeroom teacher, for support.

"Several of my students have reported teasing and bullying. A couple of the girls have cried about it," Miss Beckman replied.

It seemed this was the perfect moment to break the uncomfortable silence and introduce my proposal to create an environment of acceptance and inclusion by starting a Special Olympics team.

The principal appeared skeptical, but Miss Beckman and Mr. Thompson, the counselor, were interested and optimistic about the potential success and benefits.

In the end, they agreed to let me initiate the project. But there was little support. Because of privacy constraints, Miss Beckman couldn't give me a list of the students in her class. However, she agreed to send home a flyer describing Special Olympics and an invitation to a parent meeting for more details.

I scheduled the meeting before the Christmas break in 1978. Even though I believed in the project, I recognized I was in over my head. My doubts about my coaching abilities and knowledge of sports were evident.

Six students—five boys, including Rick and one girl—came to that first meeting with their parents. My genuine enthusiasm for helping the children feel accepted and improve their self-confidence was contagious, and their gratitude was humbling. I knew I had to bring the team to fruition and deliver on my promises.

Since there would be no funding from the school's athletic department, my first order of business was to seek donations from local organizations: the Rotary Club, the Lions Club, and the Junior Women's Club. I prepared a short slide presentation about the history of Special Olympics, followed by a talk regarding my plans for the team, current parental interest, and proposed initial expenses.

I procured enough money to order team uniforms for the six athletes, with money left over to start a savings account for the organization. The athletes needed to believe they represented Winnebago High School and deserved team uniforms.

The next step was to determine what sports the kids should compete in. Since it was the winter season, we started with bowling in February and swimming in March, and then we progressed to track and field by April.

Four more students joined our team after an article about our first bowling competition was published in the school's newsletter, naming the athletes and medals they'd won.

Bowling had been the least-challenging sport to introduce to the team; swimming was more problematic and would require additional help.

Once I acquired the pool at Rockford's Blind Center for weekly practice and had one committed volunteer to help, I still needed a male supervisor for the boys' dressing room.

"Will you come to my first swimming practice?" I asked Jeff the week before the scheduled day. "I just need someone in the boys' dressing room; you don't need to coach—unless you want to."

I worried that asking too much, too soon would be a turnoff.

"I don't know, Deb. I love your brother, and I'm comfortable around him. But I don't have the experience that you have."

"I understand. Will you come just to this first one? Otherwise, I'll have to cancel. Please? I'm working on getting more volunteers."

He knew how important this team was to me. I also knew he didn't want to disappoint me.

"Okay, I'll come to this first one," he said. "But I'm not promising anything else."

We arrived at the pool with the athletes carrying their gym bags, accompanied by one volunteer and one parent. Jeff met us at the entrance, and, after the teens welcomed him with a handshake, fist bump, or hug, I could tell he was relaxing. Their genuine enthusiasm was infectious, and Jeff's smile showed he was hooked.

My first objective was to evaluate each athlete's swimming ability. I was pleasantly relieved that they all had some basic stroke skills. Our goals would be refining each swimmer's stroke and improving their endurance to swim the pool length.

Unfortunately, that first practice wasn't without incident.

"Debbie, Debbie!" Rick screamed to me while I was helping the girls dress. "Roger is having a seizure. Jeff needs you."

Oh, no, I thought to myself. Roger's mom and his teacher had told me about his epilepsy. Despite medication, his seizures were poorly controlled, but not much could be done when he seized.

"Just stay with him until he recovers," Roger's mom had advised me.

I had debated whether to warn Jeff about the possibility that Roger might have a seizure. I'd opted not to tell him and hoped for the best.

What a surprise when I peeked into the dressing room. Jeff had instinctively positioned Roger in the recovery position, his hand gently rubbing his back. Jeff was pale but strangely calm. He caught my eye.

"You could have warned me," he said, shaking his head.

"I'm sorry; I was afraid you wouldn't agree to come or be too nervous."

"You do underestimate me," he sighed.

"I'm learning that every day." I smiled at him.

That was the turning point in Jeff's commitment to the team. It became *our* team. We planned the practices together and began to develop strategies for each athlete to succeed. Rick was our strongest swimmer, and he was willing to help the younger ones with their techniques. We would practice races by timing each heat, with the observers cheering on the swimmers.

A camaraderie was noticeably developing among the team members, and their increased self-confidence was apparent to the parents and teachers. As more articles were written about the competitions, the Special Olympic students were being recognized by their non-disabled peers. Our athletes proudly described the new interactions with kids in the hall, the high-fives and calls of "Way to go!" and "Congrats!"

The Special Olympics program far exceeded the school's expectations. But not mine. I had always been confident of its potential impact.

Each team member achieved personal growth, both physically and emotionally. They came together, awkward and shy at first, but with a desire to belong, be accepted, and have a purpose.

Rick loved introducing me as his "sister, the coach, and the boss." He thought his connection gave him importance, but his bowling and swimming achievements were notable.

Roger was the most confident initially, but his bravado was stifled if he lost a race. He eventually learned humility and more compassion toward the younger kids. Jeff became very in tune with Roger's pre-seizure aura and often could catch him as he fell to the floor.

Danny had the most apparent disability: cerebral palsy with right-side weakness. He walked with a limp and had limited mobility in his right arm. However, his deficits didn't stop Danny from trying every sport. He could swim the length of the pool, throw a strike in bowling, and shoot a free throw in basketball. Danny became my helper, keeping the stats on every member. His parents offered to care for our daughters when my mother couldn't.

Rose, the first girl to join the team, was timid, barely looked at me, and would answer questions with a one-word response. After winning her first gold medal, she blossomed. In fact, after that, she never shut up.

Tracey, the second girl to join (after Rose convinced her to), was our grumpy one. She rarely smiled, complained a lot, and just generally seemed unhappy. I gave Tracey my whistle at one practice, telling her she was in charge of starting the warm-up exercises. She couldn't hide her pleasure. After that, she asked me how she could help at every practice.

Our most entertaining athlete was Deanna, who had a vivid imagination and would tell us outlandish spy stories. She thought Jeff looked like Tom Selleck due to his curly hair and mustache, and she nicknamed him "Magnum P.I." I teased my husband that he was secretly flattered by this attention and liked the comparison.

One of our challenging members, Dwight, was on the autism spectrum. He was very bright, but his social interactions and inappropriate behavior needed improvement. By our second year, he improved significantly, and his parents were thrilled.

The tallest boy, Dale, already had basketball skills he'd learned from his brothers. One brother agreed to help us at occasional practices and competitions.

Earl, a sophomore, had a slight learning disability. He was a gifted runner, but his poor grades made him ineligible for the high-school track team. I worried when he joined our team, thinking that he'd feel uncomfortable with the more-disabled members.

"Miss Debbie, Earl just wants to run," his father told me when I expressed my concerns.

And run he did. Earl would blow out every race he was in but remained humble and sweet to all the other kids who hadn't won a medal.

Little nine-year-old Kelly really touched our hearts. She had acquired brain damage after a traumatic brain injury from a car accident, but her parents were so positive, and Kelly was a joy to coach.

Sweet Kenny was seven when we started the team and had to wait a couple of months until he turned eight to formally join our team, per the Special Olympics rules. His excitement and energy were very contagious.

The last member who made an impression was little Amy, an eight-year-old Down syndrome girl with sparkling blue eyes who wore her blond hair in braids. She was terrified of the pool and wouldn't let go of my neck for the first couple of practices. Slowly, I earned her trust, and she started kicking her legs and moving her arms. We started in the shallow end; once Amy realized she could touch the bottom, she felt comfortable paddling a few strokes. Gradually, I moved farther away from her, and her confidence grew. I didn't want to push her too much, but I hoped she could swim the 25 yards by our first meet that April.

One week before the competition, she surprised us all and swam the pool length—with no help from me. The entire team rushed to the end of the lane, screaming and jumping up and down. The girls hugged her, and the boys gave her high-fives. It was a sight to see; both Jeff and I had tears in our eyes.

Her mother was equally moved.

"You are a miracle worker," she told me.

Jeff and I continued to coach the team for three years. In 1980, we had enough boys to add a basketball team. Not wanting to leave out the girls, I thought they could be cheerleaders. After getting their sizes from the parents, I made them twirly skirts and pom-poms. Then, I recruited Roger's sister, Belinda, a former cheerleader, to teach the girls some simple cheers. The girls' parents agreed to bring them to a practice so I could surprise them with their new uniforms. Their reaction remains one of my fondest memories and another acknowledgment of this team's beneficial impact—their positive self-esteem.

The girls shrieked excitedly, trying on the skirts, jumping up and down, and twirling in circles. Tracey, the occasional sourpuss, exclaimed that it had always been her dream to be a cheerleader. She couldn't stop smiling.

We introduced the cheerleading squad at the Regionals Basketball Competition. The first cheerleaders in the history of basketball teams in the county were received very well. The Northwest District of Special Olympics president, Miss Geiger, applauded our innovation. Nearing 80, the soft-spoken woman had been my mentor, supporting my efforts from the beginning.

"This new Winnebago team may be small in numbers," she said of our newly formed team at that first meet in 1979, "but they're mighty. Do not underestimate them. The director, Debbie Miller, is determined to succeed."

Being recognized by such an accomplished, dedicated leader was an honor.

The basketball team played hard and won the final game at Regionals, qualifying the team for State games. While the boys practiced for their next competition, Belinda taught the cheerleading squad a cheer to perform at halftime. Since they had quickly learned the sideline cheers, Belinda thought the girls could learn a synchronized group-cheer routine.

She was right. They performed flawlessly and were awarded a standing ovation by the fans in the bleachers. It was a sight to behold.

By the school year of 1980-1981, the team had grown to sixteen participants. Jeff and the two other male coaches measured our success by how many medals the team won, but it was about their increased self-confidence and self-worth for me. We even added a gymnastics competition for Dwight and Amy, coached by my cousin Mary. I had accomplished what I set out to do.

It also benefited my mother in unexpected ways. She offered to help care for my girls while Jeff and I were at practice and to prepare dinner for us all when we returned. It was a tempting solution, but I needed to be sure she'd be sober and her house clean. Kelly and Jamie loved their grandmother, and I wanted to motivate my mother's sobriety and mental stability.

It worked for a few years, a win-win for everyone. Our daughters learned acceptance of people with disabilities at an early age, which resulted in their nonjudgment of others and empathy development.

"Only a life lived for others is a life worthwhile."

—Aristotle

Chapter Nine

Life-Altering Decisions

1984-1997, Illinois

After Rick graduated high school in 1981, Jeff and I resigned from coaching the Special Olympics team. Since Rick would no longer be on the team, the parents understood but were still disappointed. We celebrated the team's successes at an end-of-year picnic, and the parents expressed their gratitude by presenting us with an engraved clock.

Rick transitioned to Growth Enterprises, a sheltered workshop for developmentally disabled adults. The workshop contracted with local factories for simple piecemeal jobs that their clients were able to complete and for which they received minimal compensation. Rick enjoyed the work; his favorite was sorting, counting, and bagging small hardware items. And he was proud to be earning a paycheck.

Coaching the Special Olympics team, planning the competitions, and organizing fundraisers had taken up most of my time over the past three years. I needed a new project since Kelly and Jamie, eight and six, respectively, were in school.

A couple of part-time jobs left me bored and unfulfilled. The idea of finishing my degree in Special Education was becoming more appealing. Unfortunately, the university was too far away for a daily commute, especially with my family responsibilities.

However, a community college offered an associate's degree in nursing, and the campus was only a 30-minute drive from my home. Of course, Jeff was supportive; predictably, my mother was not.

"Why do you want to return to college now, at your age? It's a foolish idea," she admonished me. "You had your chance when you were 18."

Her words burned my heart. Our relationship had become tolerable for me, especially since she was such a good grandmother to my daughters, but she never missed an opportunity to berate or criticize me. Over the years, I received accolades from personal accomplishments, which helped my self-worth, however, not hearing anything positive from my mother was still devastating.

I chose my words carefully, realizing that if I pursued a nursing education, I would need her help with the girls. Alienating her now would not be in my best interest. She wasn't the only one who could manipulate; I learned her techniques so that I could use them to serve my interests.

"You're right, Mom. I should have finished my degree when I had the chance. But I could use your support and help with the girls now. It would mean a lot to me. I need you and love you."

"Oh, all right," she replied. "Of course, I'll help with Kelly and Jamie if you must proceed with this silly idea."

The fast-track nursing program was considered one of the toughest the college offered. The failure and dropout rate accounted for more than half of the initial admissions. Since I was an older student, it made the most sense to take the support classes the first year, before starting the demanding schedule of nursing classes and hospital clinicals.

Still, it wasn't easy for me, especially as a mother of two school-age daughters. All the classes were challenging, requiring hours of studying, leaving no extra time to do housework or be involved with the girls. Jeff helped as much as he could, but I knew I wasn't meeting my children's emotional needs. My guilt was overwhelming; I promised myself I would make it up to them once I graduated and had a less-demanding nursing position. My rationalization did nothing to appease me. I struggled with the fact that I was neglecting my girls, just as my mother had neglected me when I was small, even if my circumstances were more noble.

Money was extremely tight, with the added expense of tuition, books, and high heating bills in the winter. One of Jeff's friends gave him a wood-burning stove that he installed in the basement; since he had cut down many overgrown trees the previous summer, we had plenty of firewood. We were able to get by once Jeff switched to the evening shift for an increase in pay and using the woodstove to heat our house. Our summer garden provided enough vegetables, which I canned or froze, that would last the entire winter. It was a lot of work maintaining the garden, but it helped immensely with our frugal budget.

Despite all the rigorous demands of the nursing program and pressures at home, I graduated on the Dean's List with a GPA of 3.95. Mom did attend the pinning ceremony but never once congratulated me or said she was proud of me.

After graduation, I accepted a Neonatal Intensive Care Unit (NICU) nursing position at Rockford Memorial Hospital. I quickly realized that being a new grad in a high-risk, stressful environment wouldn't be any easier than school had been.

What was I thinking? I wondered. Or perhaps the more pertinent question was, *What was I trying to prove—and to whom? Was I still looking for my mother's approval or some validation?*

Over the next seven years, I searched for the perfect position to meet my need for a fulfilling career and a balanced home life. I hated to leave the hospital, but working weekends and holidays wasn't conducive to a happy family.

My luck changed when Rockford Memorial Hospital developed a comprehensive Pediatric Specialty outpatient clinic that included gastroenterology, pulmonology, and neurology. I interviewed with the pediatric gastroenterologist, Dr. Montes, and we hit it off immediately. He was a tall, thin, Puerto Rican with kind eyes, a comforting smile, and Spanish accent. We shared the same ideals of patient care, and his plans for the practice were exciting. He wanted his clinic nurse to have autonomy and envisioned her as an integral part of his practice.

I accepted the position and worked hard alongside Dr. Montes, learning all the pediatric GI diseases, treatments, medications, and procedures. The practice met all my needs for challenging, gratifying work. In addition to working at the clinic, I accompanied Dr. Montes on hospital rounds, assisted with procedures, and started my own gastrostomy tube clinic. Even though weekends or holidays weren't required, I still worked 50–55 hours weekly.

This meant I was still unavailable to my now-teenage daughters. They didn't seem to mind; perhaps they were comfortable with not having too much parental involvement at this stage. *Or maybe,* I thought at the time, *they'd simply gotten used to me never being home.* I prayed and hoped our relationship hadn't been damaged beyond repair, but it was a concern.

When my daughters no longer needed my mother babysitting them, she looked for something else to become involved in. Mom discovered a Special Needs Boy Scout troop, of which some of Rick's friends from Growth Enterprises were members. It was the perfect time for them to participate in a different program. Mom was excited about the prospect of working with the Scouts as they earned badges, and she enjoyed the challenge of helping Rick work through the ranks from Tenderfoot to Eagle.

This new endeavor monopolized all her time and attention, and it seemed to help her sobriety and mental stability. I wondered if the goal of Eagle had become an obsession.

Even so, her determination paid off, and, by May 1995, Rick had met all the requirements he needed to achieve the rank of Eagle. I'm not sure how much Mom had assisted him or how much of the work Rick had completed on his own, but I knew that this was her accomplishment as much as his.

I helped plan his Eagle ceremony at St. Mary's Catholic Church. More than 200 people, including family, community members, and Boy Scouts, attended his event. The townspeople came together to celebrate the little boy who had been denied Kindergarten and had gone on not only to graduate from high school but also to achieve the highest honor in Boy Scouts.

As the ceremony was about to begin, I looked for Rick to prepare him for the acceptance of his new rank. He was nowhere to be found.

"Debbie, where is Rick?" the Scoutmaster asked me. "We're ready to start."

"I'm not sure. Can you delay a few minutes while I look for him?"

I finally found him outside; he was looking up into the sky.

"Rick, what are you doing? The ceremony is about to start; you need to come inside."

"I'm waiting for Air Force One," he replied. "Bill sent me a card."

Thank you for writing to me. I always enjoy hearing from young people. You are the future of our country, and I am honored to be your President.

Bill Clinton

"Oh, Rick. I don't think he's coming; we would have heard by now. You have lots of people here, so let's go in."

"Okay, Debbie. But can we send him the video Jeff is making so he will see what he's missed?"

"Yes, Rick. We can send the video to President Clinton."

By 1996, I had worked with Dr. Montes for more than three years and still loved it. One of my proudest accomplishments was creating a support group for children and teens with inflammatory bowel diseases: ulcerative colitis and Crohn's disease. It was beneficial for the kids to talk about their feelings with each

other. As with the disabled kids in Special Olympics, children with chronic illnesses also suffer from feeling left out or different. One summer, the parents and I raised enough money selling candy bars to support a trip to a fun medical-based GI camp in Texas (Camp MAGIC), similar to camps for kids with cancer or diabetes.

At the end of January 1997, Dr. Montes called me into his office. I assumed it was to discuss the three patients he had recently admitted to the hospital.

"Debbie, I have an announcement. I've decided to accept a position at Phoenix Children's Hospital and will be leaving Rockford in August."

I was shocked into silence. The best, most-rewarding, and most-satisfying job I'd ever had was coming to an end. The old, unresolved feeling of abandonment started to grow in my gut, and a lump swelled in my throat.

"There's a nursing position for you if you want it," Dr. Montes said. "Would you and Jeff consider moving to Arizona? Debbie, you're the best nurse I've ever worked with; I'd hate to lose you. PCH would love to have you join their team."

"Uh, I, uh, I'm flattered that you have that much confidence in me," I stuttered. "But we've lived in Illinois our entire lives, and I have my mother and brother to consider."

"I understand. Talk to Jeff, and think about it. I'm unsure what will happen with our practice here or if the administration will replace me. I hope they do, for the sake of our patients. I have the contact number of the nurse manager and one of the nurses on the team if you have any questions. Of course, you'll need to fly there for an interview, but the physicians assured me it would be a formality. You have the job if you want it."

Jeff was standing at the stove, stirring pasta, when I arrived home. I hugged him and said, "I have some unexpected news. You'd better sit down."

"What's up? Good news or sad?" He was used to my different moods after work—some days, I could be excited about teaching a mom how to change her child's gastrostomy tube, or I could be terribly sad about losing a toddler with liver failure. Over the years, he could sense what I needed. Usually, it was simply listening while I vented.

"Dr. Montes is leaving Rockford. He accepted a job at a children's hospital in Arizona."

"Wow! I didn't see that coming. How will that affect your position?" he asked, assessing my reaction.

"Well, another surprising turn of events. He told me I could have a job there if I wanted, and he wondered if we would consider moving."

"Really? That sounds interesting; maybe we should think about it."

"Are you kidding? How can we leave all our families, especially my mom and Rick?" I answered, doubtful.

"Debbie, even you said the other day that you have never seen your mother this stable or happy. Rick and she are doing great. She has friends, activities, and functions. It's been years since her drinking has been an issue. And weren't you complaining about the weather just last week, saying you couldn't wait till summer? It might be nice not to have brutal winters and rainy springs."

"True. I guess it does sound tempting. But don't the logistics seem overwhelming? Moving cross-country, selling the house, and finding one in Arizona. You'll have to find a job. I can't wrap my head around it."

"There you go—worrying about stuff before it happens. We'll break it down into steps. First, we fly to Arizona so you can determine if the job is a good fit, and then we can check out neighborhoods to get a feel for the real-estate market. One step at a time. It will be an adventure; every weekend will be like a mini-vacation, exploring all the sights."

"Hmmm, when you put it that way . . . it does sound exciting."

I thought we had been in a rut, just going to work every day and spending weekends with his sister and her husband. And I have come to hate the weather in Illinois. Maybe we do need a change.

"What about the girls?" I worried they hadn't found their path or future goals since graduating. It seemed they were simply floating, without any direction, just like I was when I dropped out of college. I blamed myself for not giving them guidance when they needed it the most.

"We'll ask them to come with us. It could be a new start for them, too," he answered.

"Okay. I'll schedule the interview with the nurse manager."

We flew to Phoenix in early March. We had decided to keep our potential plans to ourselves until we decided.

The interview went well, and the entire staff made me feel welcome. The only negative was that I would have to take turns with the other two nurses, sharing on-call duties. But the Arizona weather was perfect, and we were surprised at the beauty of the desert. It wasn't the barren, colorless landscape we'd expected; the spring flowers were in full bloom, and the sky was extraordinarily blue. There were live theaters and museums, funky little ghost towns to explore, and many mountains with hiking trails.

That first night, we went to the hotel bar for a drink and started a conversation with a few locals. They had nothing negative to say about living in Phoenix except that it was hot in the summer. They were celebrating the Diamondbacks' inaugural game, which was being televised on the bar's TV. The crowd loved it. Phoenix had been waiting for a pro baseball team for years. We were caught up in the excitement and thought that it would be fun to follow the new team.

Jeff and I returned home and discussed our options. We wrote a list of pros and cons, the negatives versus the positives. Ultimately, the pros and positives outnumbered the cons and negatives, so I accepted the position, and we began our extensive moving plans.

The biggest challenge was breaking the news to my mother before the "For Sale" sign went in our front yard.

I hoped for the best.

Instead, I received a far worse reaction than I'd ever expected.

"Some of our important choices have a timeline. If we delay a decision, the opportunity is gone forever. Sometimes our doubts keep us from making a choice that involves change. Thus, an opportunity may be missed."

—James E. Faust

Chapter Ten

Arizona: *"Ditat Deus"*
God Enriches

1997-2003, Arizona

"Mom, I have exciting news," I told her on the phone. I had invited her to lunch at the Pecatonica Diner to tell her about my job offer and our plans to move, hoping that telling her in a public place would prevent an outburst. We sat down in a booth, and the waitress brought the menus.

"So, what's this big news?" she asked in a terse tone, rolling her eyes.

"I've been offered a wonderful opportunity, a nursing position at a highly rated children's hospital in Phoenix, Arizona," I told her.

I had forgotten the force of my mother's selfish narcissism. She exploded.

"If you accept this position and move," she yelled, "you will be dead to me."

I tried to calm her down.

"Mom, keep your voice down; people are looking." In our small town, everyone knew each other, and gossiping was a favorite pastime. I nodded at the couple sitting at the table by ours, but they quickly looked away, seemingly embarrassed for hearing Mom's hurtful words.

"You cannot leave me. How could you even consider this?" Her rage was palpable.

"I'm sorry, but we have decided to move."

I reached for her hand, but she pulled away, glaring at me.

"You know I love you and Rick," I continued. "And you two are doing great; you're active with the Boy Scouts and have many friends. I'll send you plane tickets so you can visit. And I'll call every week. Please, Mom—can't you be happy for me?" I begged.

She stood up, folded her arms across her chest, and repeated, "You will be dead to me."

Then she walked out. I sat there for a moment, attempting to regain my composure, but I was shaking. My mother's degree of disdain and disapproval of me could still be shocking and unexpected. I was transported back to the past as the little girl who struggled to be perfect, needing to be loved and given some approval.

Despite my mother's hurtful reaction and threats of disowning me, we moved to Phoenix. Her response was extremely unsettling, but I refused to allow her cruel manipulation destroy my happiness or future dreams anymore. I hated leaving the brother I'd cared for most of my life, but it was time.

The cross-country move was not easy, filled with several obstacles. I had to report to my new job on July 1, but we hadn't sold our house in Rockford. One of the nurses graciously allowed me to live in her house, rent-free, which helped us financially. Jeff had an opportunity to keep his employment with the Rockford Ingersoll plant but work in Mexico. Over the last decade, he had been traveling for work in several states, including Texas, Oregon, and Washington, so he was used to it. In fact, we almost moved to Oregon after he received a job offer from Boeing.

He took turns visiting me in Arizona and the girls in Illinois, alternating every two weeks. It put a lot of pressure on my 20-something-old daughters to take care of a 2400-square-foot house on three acres with an inground swimming pool and keep it presentable for realtor showings. It was way too much of a responsibility for these young adults. And once the house sold, it was up to them to pack for the move. They had justified resentment for years, adding to the indifference in our relationships even more. I wished I would've had the parental insight to have handled the situation better. But hindsight is always wiser than foresight.

Since my new job wasn't ideal from the beginning, I spent many days wondering, *What the hell did I do?* To add to the misery, the housing market in Phoenix was a seller's dream and a buyer's nightmare. I would look at a house in the morning; by that afternoon, there would be three to four offers. I was becoming desperate once we had an offer on the Rockford house. Missing my family desperately, I was becoming increasingly depressed. Finally, I found a house that had fallen out of escrow that seemed perfect. It was huge, with five bedrooms, three full baths, a family room, a formal living room, a dining room, a three-car garage, and an in-ground pool. Unfortunately, it wouldn't be completely built when my family showed up with all our belongings. I had to find a short-term lease apartment for the four of us and our 70-pound yellow lab. This was a very challenging and stressful time in our lives. And it took months for our family to recover and reconcile. I'm not sure if I ever did with my girls. But, once we finally settled into the new house, all of us enjoyed the Arizona sunshine and the moderate winter weather.

The Pediatric GI nurse position at Phoenix Children's Hospital was a means to an end. It allowed us to start a new, exciting chapter in our married life. We enjoyed discovering a foreign topography, living in a city without winters, and exploring the exciting downtown Phoenix with its new baseball stadium. Hiking the challenging peaks within the city limits became a favorite pastime.

Jeff and I fell in love with Arizona, learning about the twenty diverse ecosystems, such as the arid deserts with majestic Saguaros, river-eroded canyonlands, grass-covered plains, volcanic plateaus, and forested mountains. We made relaxing weekend trips to Northern Arizona to escape the summer's brutal temperatures. Just as Jeff had promised when we first discussed the job offer, we went on mini-vacations every chance we got. It felt like we were taking many little honeymoons we'd never had an opportunity to enjoy.

Not everything was perfect in the Grand Canyon State, though. The prestigious nursing position left me unfulfilled and dissatisfied. I no longer had a close rapport with my pediatric patients or a meaningful working relationship with Dr. Montes. Every day, I worked with a different clinic physician and assisted with hospital procedures. The other doctors couldn't match Dr. Montes' endoscopy skills, and working with them became intolerable. I hated it.

My disillusionment lasted two years until I transitioned to adult gastroenterology, working as a sedation endoscopy nurse in an outpatient clinic. The job was challenging enough, especially since I had been a pediatric nurse my entire career. It was rewarding to be screening patients for colon cancer; plus, the hours were perfect for facilitating our active, adventurous lifestyle. It was a job, not a "career," but it afforded me the chance to live a life instead of only making a living.

Otherwise, life couldn't have been better. After starting a hiking club with co-workers, we decided to plan a backpacking trip in the Grand Canyon and camp at the bottom at Phantom Ranch. Despite training for weeks, the hike was the most challenging endeavor we'd ever attempted and our most outstanding physical achievement. Something about the striped colors on the sediment walls, the blue Colorado River, and the breathtaking views was mesmerizing.

We experienced many strenuous and beautiful mountaintop hikes throughout the state, but none ever compared to our

fascination with the canyon, and we both decided that is where we would want our ashes scattered. We made three more back-packing trips, including a 26-mile rim-to-rim hike, completed in under 11 hours, and an 8-day whitewater river-rafting trip. There were other beautiful places we enjoyed exploring. We loved Sedona's brilliant red rock formations, the bustling artist

community of Jerome, the golden aspens adorning Flagstaff, and the infamous haunted inns in Prescott.

In 1997, the city of Tempe, home of Arizona State University, developed a two-mile-long man-made lake by damming a portion of the dry Salt River and adding water. It created many boating opportunities, including kayaking, rowing, outrigger paddling, and Dragon Boating, which is a traditional Chinese human-paddled watercraft activity. For races, there are 18-20 in a boat, plus a steersperson and drummer. Another co-worker convinced us to try a newly formed Dragon Boat team, and, after the first practice, we were hooked. Maria, an engaging, fiery woman from Colombia, and Louis, a quiet gay man from Puerto Rico, were the coaches. They were assembling a culturally diverse team: there were older paddlers and younger ones, a couple from India, black and brown folks. It was an incredible experience to come together and learn how to move the long boat as one. Winning our first gold medal was thrilling. Moving to Phoenix had

certainly broadened our horizons, enriching our lives in ways we never had imagined. Growing up in a small, rural, all-white town was safe and comfortable but also extremely self-limiting with its narrow-mindedness.

We became very close to Alicia, who embraced us, calling us "her Millers." She was younger than our daughters, but the generation difference didn't matter, and she became part of our family.

Our daughters eventually found their way. Jamie met a young man from New York who had recently graduated from law school, and she decided to move to Brooklyn with him.

Kelly discovered her niche in the construction/architecture industry and became very successful.

Jeff and I had never been happier, and our marriage was as strong as ever.

We were truly living our best lives.

Until I received the phone call.

"Do not let making a living prevent you from making a life."
—John Wooden

Chapter Eleven

The Promise

2003, Arizona

The sun is hot, but a misty breeze blows in from the ocean that cools the perspiration trickling on my skin, just enough to make it the perfect ambience for napping on the beach. As I slowly inhale, I take in the different smells—they seem to be in layers, like in a truffle, slightly blended, but each distinct enough to recognize. There's the salty seawater, the fragrant jasmine vine climbing on the tourist shop's side wall, the sunbather's sweet coconut oil, and the sizzling hot dogs grilling at the nearby food truck. The rhythmic sound of the waves lapping onto the shore lulls me to sleep. I feel relaxed and blissful, not a care in the world. As I drift off, I hear my husband's voice calling me . . .

"Deb, wake up. Haven't you heard me calling you?"

Jeff's voice was getting louder and more demanding. Abruptly, I was awake and slowly opened my eyes. I realized I was in my bedroom. Fuck. Desperate to return to my dreamy utopia, I rolled the pillow around my head and ignored his yelling. The pillow muffled his incessant urging, but it didn't stop.

"Debbie, you have to get up. Your brother is on the phone, and he's waiting to talk to you."

His voice was softer now, with a hint of concern, pleading with me.

"Honey, I can't stall him any longer, and he's crying," he said, pulling the pillow off my face and gently stroking my hair.

"Okay, okay. I'm awake."

My head was pounding, like it was being squeezed in a vise. I had drunk too many beers last night. Again. I'd been doing that a lot in the last few months. My life had gone from a carefree, empty-nester's to a Lifetime movie of the week. The ones that involve three hours of hopeless tragedies. Only my saga had lasted five months.

My 83-year-old mother, who had survived colon cancer less than a year ago, had been in a horrendous car accident. She suffered a neck fracture, rib fractures that caused a lung puncture and collapse, and a complex, displaced-tibia fracture. Despite a bleak prognosis, she kept on fighting.

It had been six years since Jeff and I had moved to Arizona. After the first year, Mom finally accepted my weekly phone calls, only to boast about how well Rick was doing and the lovely couple who had befriended them and become their new family. She never asked about Jeff, me, or our daughters. After experiencing her mental illness for decades, her attempts to hurt me no longer worked—I was relieved of any guilt, since they were doing well.

After my cousin called about Mom's accident, I spoke to the trauma surgeon, who informed me he was taking her to surgery to stabilize the precarious neck fracture. He bluntly reported that he didn't expect her to last the night.

To everyone's surprise, she did.

Jeff surprised me with a sizable cash-out from his 401(k) to fund a leave of absence from my work, so that I could fly to Illinois and assess my mother's and brother's situation.

"How could you do this without discussing it with me first?" I asked angrily. "What about our retirement?"

"Because I knew you would disagree. Debbie, you need to go. I don't want you to worry about money."

"I know you're right. I'm just . . . so . . ." *My cousin, Trish, had been taking care of everything—for weeks—and I felt like I was taking advantage of her kindness and feelings of family obligation. I needed to go.*

I blubbered, not finding the words to express my feelings.

"Thank you," I finally said. I felt I didn't deserve this selfless, generous, loving man who always prioritized my needs.

My nursing experience didn't prepare me for the sight of Mom's frail body. It was hard not to feel pity, seeing her with a halo cage screwed to her scalp and a frightening metal retractor attached to her leg. She was hooked up to monitors and IVs, with tubes and wires everywhere.

All my painful, angry, and hurtful feelings were replaced with compassion and concern for her. After all, she still was my mother and needed me again. Being a nurse was not only my profession; it was my identity. I had taken the Florence Nightingale Pledge, promising to care for all patients.

Mom reached for my hand as I sat next to her bed.

"You came," she said, tears streaming down her cheeks.

"Of course," was all I could say.

After a month, she was stable enough to be transferred to a skilled nursing facility, although her quality of life was nil. She had a tracheotomy, a gastrostomy tube, an ostomy bag, and a urinary catheter. I pleaded with the neurosurgeon to remove the halo for her comfort, but she refused because the neck fracture had failed to heal. She warned me that one abrupt move, such as a sneeze, could be fatal.

"Would that be a bad thing?" I asked. "Look at her." She had not been able to change position for weeks.

The neurosurgeon finally conceded to a soft neck collar if I signed a no-fault clause, promising not to sue in the event of her death.

My cousin Mary, who's an attorney, called me one night after I'd left the nursing facility.

"Debbie, I heard some gossip about your mother," she said. "There are rumors that she changed her will after you moved to Arizona and used a lawyer who I know has no experience with trusts. If I were you, I'd try to find that will before you leave."

I went through Mom's desk and found the will. Sure enough, she had named two non-family members as executors, with no provisions for Rick's care in a trust. I was livid. I called my cousin back and asked for a referral to a trust attorney.

The following day, I shoved the will in Mom's face.

"What the hell is this? Do you realize what you've done? You really think these guys will take care of Rick? They just want your house."

She turned away, avoiding my eyes. Then, she whispered, "I was angry that you left us. They seemed like they cared."

"Well, your vengeance will not hurt me this time. Your hateful, vindictive revenge will hurt only your son. I'm hiring an attorney who specializes in Special Needs Irrevocable Trusts. Anything left in your estate after paying outstanding medical bills will go into a trust solely for Rick's care. Do you understand? And you *will* sign it, naming me as the trustee. I will always take care of Ricky."

She nodded, as she started to cry.

"I'll be back tomorrow with the attorney."

After weeks of exhausting every family member and friends to take care of Rick and drive him to work, I placed him in a group home, with Trish's assistance. It seemed the best, most practical solution under the circumstances. He could maintain his routine, keep his job at Growth Enterprises, and continue visiting Mom. Since there wasn't anything more I could accomplish, I returned to Arizona but continued to manage care for both Rick and my mother from afar, with daily phone calls to Mom's nursing facility and Rick's group home.

The couple of beers each night numbed my emotional distress.

But alcohol didn't solve my problems. And I was painfully aware that it was necessary to keep it in check, considering my genetics.

Rick was calling from the group home, and Jeff couldn't delay him any longer. I shuddered at the thought of what he might need and tried to hide my annoyance.

"Hi, Ricky. What's up?" I said, attempting to sound cheerful, even though my head felt like it would explode.

"Hi, Deb."

He began to sob uncontrollably, making his words incomprehensible.

"Sweetie, try to calm down, and tell me what's wrong," I said, trying to comfort him.

"I can't take it anymore. Can I come live with you and Jeff? I need family."

"Oh, Rick, are you sure? I thought you liked living there. And what about Mom? Won't you miss seeing her?"

"No," he answered defiantly. "I don't like it here. I don't want to see Mom anymore. She's not the same. She doesn't talk to me. Last night, when I said my prayers, I told God he could have her. I'm sad. Please, Debbie, can I come live with you? I be good. Please."

He began crying again.

"Okay, Rick. Try to stop crying. Of course, you can come here if that's what you want," I told him, trying to sound convincing but not knowing how I would arrange it—or if I wanted to.

"Can I come tomorrow?" he asked, excitedly.

"No, not tomorrow. We have lots of stuff to figure out, and it will take Jeff a couple of days to drive there. So, you need to be patient."

"Okay, Debbie. I'll be patient, but you promise. Right?"

"Yes, I promise. We'll come get you."

"I love you, Debbie."

"I love you, too. Rick."

"Okay, bye. I gotta go."

I sat for a moment, collecting my thoughts. Then I fell to my knees, crying hysterically.

I love my brother, but did that mean I had to give up my life? Again? Hadn't I already sacrificed my entire childhood taking care of him when our mother couldn't? Most of my adolescence and adult life was spent stepping in for my mother, being Rick's advocate. When will my life be my own?

The Promise

Then I remembered my secret promise to him when I was ten: I would always protect him.

Jeff's and my six-year honeymoon was over. We would be solely responsible for my brother, who would need us for the rest of his life.

Jeff came up the stairs and held me close, without saying a word, until my tears stopped. He looked at me and smiled.

"I'll leave in the morning. It'll be all right. I promise."

"The greatest glory in living lies not in never falling, but in rising every time we fall."

—Nelson Mandela

Chapter Twelve

The Saga Ends

2004, Arizona

Jeff and Rick were exhausted after making the 1800-mile, two-day-long drive. They arrived home in mid-January.

"How was Mom when you told her we were moving Rick to Arizona?" I asked Jeff. I was relieved I hadn't been the one to break the news to her, assuming she would take it better from my husband.

"She smiled, thanked me, and cried a little when Rick hugged her goodbye. I believe she knows it's his best option. Your mom is becoming weaker. She kept nodding off; I don't think it will be long."

The next few weeks were spent adjusting to our new living arrangement, with the three of us. I knew Rick could be more independent, and I planned to introduce new skills slowly, not to overwhelm him. We started with making his bed and placing his dirty clothes in the hamper. Mom never taught him simple tasks because household chores were never her priority.

We progressed to teaching him how to do his laundry, placing dishes in the dishwasher, and cleaning his room. He was proud of his accomplishments since we'd made a big deal about his contributions to our family.

I made an appointment for him with my primary-care physician. He was significantly overweight, close to 200 pounds at five-foot-two. I was also concerned about his high cholesterol and low thyroid levels. He began losing weight after starting medications, eating healthy meals, with controlled portions, and beginning a walking routine.

Before Mom's accident, Rick had a busy life filled with activities. He worked five days a week at Growth Enterprises, attended Boy Scout meetings in the evenings, and was involved with various weekend functions. After reaching the rank of Eagle Scout, he was promoted to Junior Troop Leader and helped with the organization's leadership duties.

My biggest concern in moving him to Arizona and having him live with us was a lack of peer socialization. I took a couple of weeks off from my job to get him acclimated to his surroundings and new routine, but he needed something to keep him occupied and a sense of purpose for when Jeff and I returned to work. We lived in Cave Creek, a smaller town north of Phoenix. Unfortunately, there were no services for developmentally disabled adults in the area.

The job counselor at Growth Enterprises had encouraged Mom over the years to consider Rick's employment outside the sheltered workshop. He felt Rick could work in the community, possibly as a grocery bagger. But Mom wasn't comfortable exposing Rick to the potential risk of mistreatment or prejudice in the world. However, she did allow him to take "job training" classes that included interviewing skills and filling out job applications.

"Debbie, look at this application your brother filled out," she'd said at the time, shoving the paperwork at me. I noted Rick's neat printing as I scanned the document. He had filled in the correct age in the blank provided, but where "sex" was listed, he had written "No" instead of "Male."

"Oh, Mom." I started laughing hysterically and couldn't stop despite her complaints. "You must admit that's pretty funny. At least he didn't write 'yes' or 'not yet.'"

This humorous memory came to me one day as I picked up a few things at the local grocery store, only two blocks from our house. *Maybe Rick could work here,* I thought. *It's close enough for him to walk to.*

I asked to speak to the store manager to discuss possible employment for my brother. Miss Adams was a tall, formidable woman, somewhat intimidating. She seemed to be in a hurry as she let me into her office and appeared skeptical when I explained my brother's Down-syndrome diagnosis, even though I emphasized his high-functioning abilities.

"I'm not sure, Mrs. Miller. I've heard other stores in the valley have successfully hired special-needs employees, but your brother would be the first and only one at this branch."

She sounded increasingly less optimistic. *Maybe,* I thought, *she was trying to dissuade me.*

I took her response as a challenge.

"Would you please interview him?" I asked. "And if you don't think he'd be an asset, I'll understand."

"Okay," she replied, rolling her eyes, not even bothering to hide her annoyance. "Have him come tomorrow at two."

"Thank you," I said, standing up and shaking her hand. "You won't be disappointed."

That evening at dinner, Jeff and I prepared Rick for the interview, telling him to listen carefully to the questions and answer slowly. I chose khaki slacks and a button-down shirt for him to wear the next day. Much to my surprise, he came out of his room wearing his blue suit.

"Rick, you don't need to wear a suit."

"Well, we were taught at Growth Enterprises that you must dress for the part, and a suit is the right thing to wear for a job interview," he replied confidently.

At the interview, Rick politely shook Miss Adams's hand as we entered her office. "I'm Rick," he said. I could tell she was impressed with him already. But she needed to be sure he could handle direction without me, so I waited outside. They both had huge smiles when they came out.

"Debbie, I got the job." Rick excitedly announced.

"You were right, Mrs. Miller—he's very impressive. I'm happy for him to join the team." Her previous impersonal demeanor had softened.

As I had done with my daughters when they walked to school on their first day, I walked the route with Rick, showing him the crosswalk button and then secretly following behind him until I was confident he could cross the busy street safely.

Rick didn't take long to learn the duties of a courtesy clerk. He methodically bagged the customers' groceries, understanding how to place the heavy items on the bottom to minimize breakage and the bakery products on top to prevent crushing. His team leader worried that his slow pace would be a problem with impatient customers, but the opposite occurred. Rick's line was the longest, but not because it was the slowest. On the contrary, many people preferred his line so they could say, "Hi," "Thanks," and "Good job!" He was becoming a very popular courtesy clerk. If Jeff or I stopped in, Rick had to proudly introduce us to all the staff and any close-by customers. The cashiers complimented his work ethic and diligent attention to detail.

In March, Vicki, my co-worker, and her husband invited us to a Renaissance Festival in Mesa, close to the Superstition Mountains. The comedy shows and raptor presentation were our favorites, but Rick loved the huge turkey leg the best. On the way home, I turned my phone back on to find several missed voicemails from Mom's nursing facility and Rockford Memorial Hospital.

Mom had been transferred to the hospital and admitted to the ICU with a fever and respiratory distress.

"Your mother is critically ill," the physician told me.

"She has been for months," I said. "What's changed?"

"She has an acute respiratory infection, which is compromising her airway. We may have to put her on a ventilator."

"Absolutely not—you do know she is a DNR?" I demanded.

"Okay, we will administer comfort measures only, treat the infection with antibiotics, and keep her hydrated." The physician understood.

"Thank you. I'll call in the morning, but please call if there are any significant changes. You realize I'm in Arizona; I'll try to get there soon."

I decided to tell Rick that Mom had to go to the hospital because she was sicker. I didn't think he would understand the difference in facilities or that the hospital meant "acute" versus "stable."

But when he asked, "Is she going to die, Debbie?" I thought, *Maybe he* does *understand.* He seemed to have a unique perception and intuition.

I was awakened in the early morning hours by a call from the hospital.

"Mrs. Miller." I didn't recognize this physician's voice. "I need your permission to place your mother on a ventilator."

"I already addressed this last night," I said. "No ventilator, just comfort."

"Your mother won't survive the day," the young doctor replied.

"And that will be the best possible outcome at this point. Can you imagine the agony and suffering she's endured for the past several months? Need I remind you of your oath, 'First, do no harm'? Please, just make her comfortable and give her peace. I need to call family to go be with her."

I hung up the phone.

I kept my composure while I called Nancy, our oldest family friend. She and my half-brother had dated in high school; she'd been Mom's choice for Rod's wife, and she was my godmother; Mom still loved her. Nancy had known me since I was a little girl and had been a part of every celebratory occasion and tragic event. Since she was in nursing school when Ricky was born, she recognized his diagnosis before my parents were informed. While Rick was still in the group home, she had orchestrated a carpooling group to take him to his work and to the hospital to visit Mom. She is the epitome of selfless friendship, continuously going above and beyond, and I have loved her all my life.

"Nancy, it's Deb," I said, trying not to cry.

"Oh, honey. I was thinking of calling you. How's your mom? I haven't seen her for a couple of days; it's been so busy in the office."

"Uh, that's why I'm calling. It's time. Can you go be with her? She's in the ICU at Rockford Memorial Hospital. The doctor thinks she'll pass in the next few hours. I don't want her to be alone."

"Of course. I'll go right now and call you later."

On March 15, 2004, my mother peacefully passed away after suffering for seven months. Rick took the news better than I expected. He even said a few words at the funeral when I could not.

It took us two weeks to clear the house and get it ready to sell. Mother's hoarding had worsened; every room and closet was packed with stuff, clothes, magazines, craft items, and mostly junk. I appreciated the help from Rod and one of his sons, as it was a difficult, dirty job.

Driving back to Arizona, after all the end-of-life details had been completed, I could finally confront my feelings about my mother's death. I had shed a few tears when Rick spoke at the service; other than that, I felt only ambivalence. I was relieved that she was no longer suffering, just as I would care about any patient. But there were no feelings of profound loss or sadness, anger or bitterness, only emotional numbness.

Creating an invisible shield to protect me from her personal attacks had served me well over the years.

The saga was over.

And I was free.

"Strength does not come from winning. Your struggles develop your strengths. When you go through hardships and decide not to surrender, that is strength."

—Arnold Schwarzenegger

Chapter Thirteen

The Jellybean Conspiracy

2005, Arizona

Rick did well with his work schedule and chores; he made his bed every morning and kept his room tidy. But I still worried about his lack of socialization. We tried to compensate by doing fun activities or sightseeing on the weekends.

Continuing to search for programs that would give him peer engagement, I discovered the Association for Retarded Citizens (ARC) in Tempe. The ARC of Tempe's mission statement spoke to me: *To create equality with people with intellectual and developmental disabilities through advocacy, education, and social opportunities.* The word "retarded" in their name was cringeworthy, but the group was known mainly by the acronym "ARC."

I spoke with the director about the program's activities and schedule, and took some vacation days so Rick could check it out. He loved it. It had a full program in the evenings during the week and on Saturday mornings. Some activities charged a small fee, but many were free, as was the dinner meal, which was included in the reasonable monthly dues. They also planned a few major outings throughout the year, such as a trip to Disneyland. There was just one problem: the ARC was 40 minutes away from our home, and the program started at 4 p.m., 90 minutes before either Jeff or I got home. Our local public transportation didn't come as far north as Cave Creek.

It was extremely frustrating to have found an outstanding program for my brother but no way to get him there. However, I never quit easily when it came to advocating for my brother.

Perhaps public awareness about the lack of transportation services for people with disabilities was needed, I thought. After all, the Americans with Disabilities Act (ADA) had been passed in 1990, imposing accessibility requirements on public accommodations. I was unsure if it applied to our situation, so I wrote to a columnist on the editorial page of *The Arizona Republic,* the state's daily paper, for direction. Laurie Roberts had written several special-interest stories that were inspiring. She responded to my letter right away and asked to interview Rick and me for an article about our dilemma.

Laurie was very comfortable talking with Rick and seemed touched by his life story. She wrote a compelling piece about our journey and how the ARC program could be important for Rick's socialization if not for the transportation barrier. The response was positive, with four people volunteering to drive him, creating a carpool, and allowing him to attend the ARC two or three days per week. Over the next two years, the three men and one woman were not only Rick's drivers, but they also became our close friends. These unexpected relationships happened because of Laurie's article. I learned that ordinary people could do extraordinary things to make a difference in everyday lives. It gave me a renewed faith in humanity.

The Down Syndrome Network of Arizona was another group I stumbled upon while conducting my research. It was still in its infancy, having started in 2002, and was primarily involved in supporting new parents of Down syndrome babies. The directors were very kind but didn't have much to offer me as the sister of an adult with Down syndrome.

Instead, I became a positive role model for the parents of young children with DS, showing what my brother had achieved, despite being born before special education and services. I reassured them that the future was bright for their children because they had many more advantages.

One month, the DS Network newsletter printed an advertisement for the Fountain Hills Youth Theatre, asking for Down-syndrome teens to audition for a part in their upcoming production, *The Jellybean Conspiracy*. The play centered around a high-school girl, Cricket, who was embarrassed about her Down-syndrome brother, Tom, and wanted to keep him from her classmates.

This is my life, I remember thinking at the time. *Despite advocating for and supporting my brother for most of my life, sometimes he did embarrass me.* That was a difficult emotion to admit, but maybe that was also just being human.

Even though Rick wasn't a teen, I knew he could pass for one, so I signed him up for the audition.

The youth theater director, Ross Collins, warmly welcomed us as we entered the auditorium. The teen actors looked at us suspiciously, as if they'd never seen someone with Down syndrome. They kept their distance, except for Shelley, who had been cast to play the role of Tom's sister. She introduced herself to Rick, showing no fear, and started talking to him about her music favorites, sharing her earbuds with him so he could hear her tunes. Seeing how readily she accepted Rick as her peer was sweet to observe. Shelley had a completely natural and easygoing way with him. It helped the other cast members' acceptance of Rick.

Rick aced the audition, following directions perfectly and displaying convincing emotion when asked. Even I was amazed at his performing ability.

Director Collins presented the obligations for rehearsals and the productions if Rick accepted the role of Tom. It was an intensive, laborious schedule to commit to, but I reasoned that it would be only six weeks out of my life. We were all exhausted by the end, but watching the dress rehearsal energized all of us.

The positive results—for everyone involved—outweighed any extra effort on my part. The other actors' concerns were alleviated as the weeks progressed, because Rick came to every rehearsal prepared. I rehearsed with him every day, and he learned his few lines quickly.

In addition to memorizing his lines, he had to learn some simple tap-dance steps. That proved more of a challenge for him, but he eventually was able to execute the steps flawlessly.

We were all nervous on opening night. A couple of cast members and I were concerned that Rick might not be able to pull off a performance in front of a packed audience. But Ross and Shelley believed Rick would be fine. He did amazingly well at the dress rehearsal.

What if he froze or forgot his lines? I wondered.

Ross had prepared the other actors how to react and compensate in that scenario. And, to everyone's surprise and delight, Rick executed a Tony-Award-worthy performance. The audience showed their approval with a standing ovation.

As Rick's sister, I had experienced many proud moments throughout his life. I'd seen him graduate from high school, win medals in Special Olympics, and achieve the Eagle Scout rank in Boy Scouts.

But watching him perform skillfully in a play with typical teen actors became one of my most incredible memories.

A few months later, Ross called me.

"Debbie, Rick was nominated for the AriZoni Award!" he announced. "I think he could win it. He should wear a tux to the ceremony."

The AriZoni Award was Phoenix's version of the Tony Awards. Both Rick and Shelley were nominated, as were the play and Ross for its direction.

Due to Mr. Collins's recommendation, I took Rick to Men's Wearhouse® for a tuxedo rental. The salesman was impressed as Rick bragged about his performance.

The awards ceremony was exciting. It was fun watching people dressed in their finest attire and listening as the nominations were announced and the winners accepted their awards.

Then, the time came for the youth-theater nominations. When Rick was announced as the winner of Best Guest Actor, I worried—just as I had when we were children—about what he would say as he accepted the award.

Would he embarrass me?

I held my breath as I watched him confidently walk up the steps to the stage and face the audience. Like a Broadway actor, he thanked his fellow performers, the stage crew, and the director for helping him.

Then he raised the plaque to the sky and said, "This is for you, Mom."

Everyone in the audience stood and erupted in applause and cheers.

Of course, I was thrilled for him. But I had a nagging thought that I wasn't proud of; nevertheless, it was there. I had spent five days per week, for six weeks, driving Rick to play practice after working nine hours and on Saturday morning, my day off. And I spent hours rehearsing his lines with him.

He thanked everyone in the play, even his dead mother. But not me.

I felt used, unappreciated, even somewhat angry. My brother had always gotten special attention.

What is wrong with me? I thought—just another one of my unresolved feelings of resentment entangled with obligation.

I had become a believable actor as I smiled and accompanied Rick to the cast party. Of course, I was proud of him. But I wondered if my personal identity as my brother's sister was the only thing that I would be known for.

Still, the amazing relationships I have made and heartfelt humanity I have experienced by being his sister during my life have been amazing. It has made any sacrifices worthwhile.

I wrote this poem for the play's program:

He's My Brother

Rick, who plays Tom, is my real-life brother

"Pioneers," they were called, our father and mother
They said "NO" to an institution. "We won't send
him away."
The doctors replied, "What about your daughter—do
you dare?"
"Yes," they cried. "He'll teach her to be strong, to fight,
and to care."

Without any resources, no PT or speech
Developmental milestones and goals he did reach
The doctors were wrong; Rick did walk and talk.
And as you can see, he is very bright.
Unlike Tom, he can read and write.

Growing up in the '60s was not easy.
There was no acceptance, only ignorance and pity.
Harsh words and prejudice were endured.
As a teen, I felt like Cricket, thinking life was unfair.
But, as my parents predicted, I did learn to care.

Our parents have since passed, and Rick lives with me.
True acceptance takes time and maturity.
We feel truly blessed, for he has taught us many things
Patience, compassion, and a sense of humor, too.
Strength, empathy, and love that is true.

Raising Ricky

"Unconditional love means not expecting anything in return
but cherishing the happiness of the person you love."
—Thich Nhat Hanh
True Love: A Practice for Awakening the Heart (1997)

Chapter Fourteen

Apartment Life and Adolescent Behavior

2006-2015, Arizona

In addition to social activities, the ARC offered indepen-dent-living-skills classes. The director felt Rick could live relatively independently, with some assistance and supervision. She assisted us in finding a suitable roommate for Rick so we could pursue the prospect of him living in an apartment within walking distance of the ARC.

We met Ron and his parents to discuss budgets, potential living expenses, and necessary household furnishings. After the rent amount was agreed upon, we found an apartment complex close enough to the ARC and less than a block from a Safeway grocery store, the same chain Rick had worked at in Cave Creek. The location was ideal, and the apartment managers were very accepting of renting to developmentally disabled young men. I had already talked with the Safeway manager about transferring Rick to the Tempe store.

Still, I was concerned about the boys' compatibility. They had completely different personalities; Ron had a flat affect and spoke in a dull monotone without emotion. His elderly parents were anxious for him to be independent and give them time for themselves.

They were impressed with Rick's outgoing, engaging disposition and thought his sunny demeanor would be helpful to their son. I had my doubts, but the arrangement had too many positive aspects not to consider a trial period.

We started with a month-to-month lease and then went to a year after the first six months went well. Initially, there were only a few common roommate issues; Rick complained that Ron was eating his food, which was resolved by purchasing a small dorm refrigerator for his room. Rick also reported that Ron wasn't helping with the cleaning, so I contacted Ron's mom. Instead of encouraging Ron to share the household chores, she cleaned the apartment herself. She also would do all of Ron's laundry. Her idea of independent living differed from mine.

I made bimonthly visits to the apartment for grocery shopping and setting up Rick's allowance. Instead of trusting him with a debit or credit card, I placed cash in labeled envelopes for designated ARC activities and his laundry. He did his laundry at the apartment facility, fixed easy meals, and was incredibly proud of himself, just as I was. We had no significant issues for the first three years.

We had purchased a cell phone for Rick, with limited minutes, to use in emergencies. One day, he phoned me.

"Debbie, I have good news; Ron and I will have healthy water."

"What?" I asked. "Healthy water? What are you talking about?"

"The man told us how bad our water is and wanted to help us."

"Rick, what man?" I was becoming concerned.

"The man at the door," he answered.

My biggest fear of him living independently had just become real. Trying to stay calm, I lowered my voice.

"Rick, did you let a stranger into the apartment?"

"Not a stranger," he replied. "He told Ron his name and gave us a card. And he cares about our health. He was nice."

Rick was getting defensive, so I knew I should change my tone to learn what happened.

"Okay, tell me about it."

I finally got to the bottom of the story. A salesman selling water-purification systems knocked on the boys' door, and Ron let him in. He told the boys that the city water was dirty and could make them sick. But he could sell them a system that would give them healthy water. The salesman knew the boys had an intellectual disability and took advantage of them by preying on their gullibility.

Ron paid a down payment for the system with his debit card and signed the contract, agreeing to monthly installments. I called his parents, who became so upset that they didn't know what to do, so I volunteered to handle the situation.

I called the company, spoke to the manager, and explained how this salesman had taken advantage of the boys. I demanded that the contract be canceled, and all money be refunded to Ron's card. If not, I threatened to sue for fraud and take the story to the media. I knew Laurie, the reporter who wrote the previous story about Rick, would love to expose this exploitation of two young men with special needs.

"Oh, Miss, that won't be necessary," the manager promised. "Of course, we'll cancel the contract and fire the salesman for his fraudulent actions."

Ron's brother Dan was a Tempe cop, and he and I had a serious talk with the boys about "Stranger Danger" and not opening the door or talking to strangers. It was a difficult conversation; we hated to crush their trusting, kindhearted worldview. But their safety and potential vulnerability were our immediate concerns. We also spoke to the apartment manager, who was equally disturbed about the incident and reinforced the no-solicitation policy; we put a "No Solicitation" sign on their door and asked their friendly neighbor to check in on them occasionally.

Rick's phone bills had been consistent for three years and then abruptly went up to $200 in overages, with one unrecognizable number other than mine listed on his monthly bill.

"Your bill was high this month," I told him. "Who are you calling?"

"My new friend," he answered. "We're good buddies."

"That's nice, Rick. But your phone is for emergencies only, or you can call me if necessary. Your budget doesn't allow for this."

His monthly Social Security check covered his rent, groceries, and utilities but left little for much else; his Safeway paycheck helped with the ARC dues and activities that required a fee.

I tried to explain to Rick that we couldn't afford a phone bill this high and that I would pay it this month, but if it continued, he would lose his phone.

"Okay, I'm sorry. I gotta go." He was in a hurry to get off the phone.

The following month, the bill was even higher. "Rick, I'm very disappointed. Your phone bill is higher than last month's. I'm taking your phone, and you will be grounded from the ARC for a week. Do you understand?"

He started crying and said, "I'm sorry. I won't do it again. Can I go bowling next week?"

He didn't sound sincere, and it felt like a different attitude was emerging.

The following week, Ron's mom called, saying that Rick's new friend was spending the night at the apartment a couple of times a week, and they were staying up till early morning. She also said they didn't include Ron in their video-game playing. I knew nothing about this new friend spending the night.

I called the ARC director.

"Julie, is something going on with Rick?"

"Um, yeah, I've been meaning to call you. We have a new participant, John, who has a discipline problem. He's having a negative influence on Rick. I hesitated to contact you due to privacy rules, but both boys' behavior is unacceptable. Rick has even been rude to other members and staff, and he's been missing days here. Ron told us that Rick and John stay up all night playing video games."

"Oh, my. He's never acted out like this. I'm shocked and very disappointed. What about the boy's parents?" I asked.

"They don't seem to care about John's behavior. I even warned them of suspension if it continued. The staff is worried about Rick; he's acting totally out of character."

"You can be assured this will end today," I promised her. "We'll pick him up tomorrow for a weekend home visit. It's time for consequences."

Jeff and I were waiting in the ARC parking lot when Rick and the new boy walked out. He looked surprised as I called him over.

"Hi, Rick." I smiled. "Where's Ron? We'll give you boys a ride home," I said, ignoring John.

"What about John? He was coming home with me."

"Not this time. You're coming home with us for the weekend."

"But why?" he asked, looking puzzled. "I want to stay here."

"Because Jeff and I need to talk with you."

Rick looked back at John and then at us; he shrugged his shoulders and got into our car. We took Ron and him back to their apartment so Rick could pack a bag for the weekend.

My attempts at small talk during the ride to our house were met with silence from Rick. His arms were crossed in front of his chest, as he pouted.

Given Rick's smug attitude and defiant reactions, I realized I was entering unfamiliar territory and needed to tread carefully. He had always been agreeable and wanted to please everyone. The only time he had acted out was in high school, due to bullying. And now he was in his 40s, exhibiting adolescent rebellion.

I decided to wait until after dinner for our talk, allowing Rick to get settled and comfortable.

"You want to play 'Wii' with me?" I asked. "We got a new game."

"You bet," he answered excitedly. Rick and I played while Jeff grilled hamburgers outside on the patio.

I started the conversation by asking about his job, his activities, and the big trip to Disneyland that was being planned next month through the ARC. Then, I asked about John.

"Tell me about the new participant, John."

Rick looked down and started fidgeting with his hands, looking guilty about something.

"He's fun," he finally answered so quietly I could barely hear him.

"Rick, I talked with Julie. She told me some not-very-nice things about John. And she also told me about how you've been acting."

He started crying and saying he was sorry.

"Can you tell me what you're sorry about?" I needed to know if he understood how his behavior was unacceptable. He admitted to not listening to the ARC staff and not being nice.

"Has John been staying overnight at the apartment?"

"Um, yeah. Is that okay?" Rick asked.

"No, Rick, it is not. That's not being fair to Ron, your roommate. Julie told me that you've been missing days at the ARC. John is no longer allowed to stay overnight. Do you understand? What about your phone bill? You promised me that you would stop calling people."

"Debbie, I did. But John keeps calling me," he explained. He then started crying again.

"All right, Rick. Calm down. But this is serious. Julie may have to suspend John from the ARC, and if you continue to behave like him, she will suspend you, too."

That made the impression I was looking for. He seemed to understand the significance of his negative behavior.

We finished dinner, and then the three of us played Wii until bedtime, which lightened the mood. Rick was more relaxed and happier, laughing a lot.

The following morning, he returned to his old self, talkative and engaging.

"Welcome back, Ricky," Jeff told him as they hugged.

I decided to call John's mother about our concerns to explain why I needed to block John's number from Rick's cell phone and let her know that sleepovers were not allowed. Her tone was contentious, but she agreed to tell John.

"Is it okay for Rick to come to our house?" she asked sarcastically. "He's such a good influence for John."

"Well, the opposite is happening; Rick has been acting out since they became friends. If his negative behavior continues, the answer is 'No,'" I told her bluntly.

Julie informed me she had to expel John from the ARC the following month. The staff overheard Rick telling him that he wasn't acting nice. John got mad, started throwing things, and a book hit one of the participants.

I felt terrible for the young man. *There must be serious problems in the home,* I reasoned. But John's anger could not be ignored.

Certainly, Rick wasn't perfect, but most of the latent adolescent rebellion could be addressed with simple consequences. His Safeway paycheck was directly deposited into our co-owned checking account, but the last few checks had been considerably smaller.

"Rick, why aren't you getting your regular hours?" I asked him.

When he'd transferred to the Tempe store, we gave the manager Rick's available days and hours, requesting a minimum of six to eight days in a two-week pay period. We needed that much to cover the extra ARC expenses.

"I don't know," he replied.

"Rick, can you talk to the manager? You really need the same hours to participate in the ARC."

"Okay, I will," he promised.

The next check was no different. He'd worked only three days that pay period, and I was worried about him having too much free time. When I took Rick to the store to speak to the manager, he seemed nervous. The manager said that it was Rick who had requested fewer hours.

I tried to hide my disappointment and dismay with my brother, who had lied to me.

"Rick, you have a choice. If you want to attend ARC activities with a fee, you must work at least three days per week. Or you can only attend the free nights."

"Okay, I'll work more," Rick finally answered. He turned to his manager. "I'm sorry, Mr. Webster."

Best Buddies, a program that builds one-on-one friendships between people with and without intellectual and developmental disabilities, came to the ARC to present their initiative of matching Best Buddies with ARC members. It offered social interactions while improving the quality of life and level of inclusion. Rick was assigned a buddy named Ryan, an ASU student. Ryan was a good match for him.

They started hanging out, going to movies, and getting to know each other. Soon, Ryan had ambitious goals for my brother. He wanted to get involved in the "Spread the Word to End the Word," a campaign to raise awareness of the hurtful effects of the words "retard" and "retarded," and encourage people to pledge to stop using them.

Ryan worked with Rick on speeches about the harmful effects of using the "R" word in casual conversation. Most people had no idea that this common utterance was hurtful to people with developmental disabilities. Rick was able to deliver his speeches fairly eloquently, with few stammers, and was received very well at local high schools.

When Rick's 50th birthday was nearing, I received a call from Michele, from the Arizona Down Syndrome Network, who wanted to plan a surprise birthday party for him. They wanted to honor and recognize an accomplished adult with Down syndrome. She said that they would handle everything, from obtaining the venue, to food and entertainment. All I had to do was get him to the location without his awareness and let them know of any people I wanted to invite. It was an epic event, with more than 100 people attending, including ARC participants, *The Jellybean Conspiracy* director and cast, Best Buddies, and many family members and friends. Of course, he made an impressive, but humble, speech. Once again, I was reminded of the hundreds of people his life had touched and how fortunate I was to be his sister.

However, Rick's public good work sometimes clashed with his personal life. The recent issues with John and Rick's behavior still bothered Rick's roommate, Ron, and his parents.

Probably the most devious stunt Rick pulled during his nine years in the apartment was also the most unbelievable.

Dan, Ron's brother, called me with an outlandish story. Ron had received a large-screen TV for Christmas, and his parents had placed the older TV in his closet.

While Ron was at work, Rick stole the smaller TV, put it in a Safeway shopping cart, and took it to a pawn shop in a strip mall across the street from his apartment complex.

It was hard to believe that he had calculated a plan to pawn Ron's TV.

How did he even know what a pawn shop was? I wondered.

The irony was Rick had seen the shop on his way to church and read the writing on the window: "Money for your stuff." He reasoned that Ron wasn't using the TV, so why not sell it?

I was getting to the end of my rope and started thinking about placing Rick in another group home, here in Arizona.

Jeff said he'd handle it. He visited the apartment and took Rick to buy back the TV from the pawn shop, which cost more than the money he'd received for it. At least losing money was some punishment. I wasn't sure if Rick comprehended that he'd done anything wrong or that stealing was a crime. But I knew how I felt; not only was I disappointed—I was also ashamed of his behavior. However, I wondered if my expectations were unreasonable.

Ron's parents were understandably upset and threatened to move Ron out of the apartment. The brother calmed them down by putting a lock on Ron's bedroom that could be locked from the outside. That appeased them, however, their trust in Rick was lost.

It wasn't surprising, but it was suspicious when, at the end of the year's lease, Dan called to let us know that Ron had lost his job and would be moving out at the end of the month.

Since we couldn't afford Rick's apartment without a room-mate, we moved him back to our house. This was another problematic adjustment for us, because Rick had been relatively independent for nine years and lately had been having behavior and attitude issues.

Now that Jeff was retired and home, I worried about increased tension. We had been losing our patience with Rick and wondered about different lifestyle options for all of us. One idea that we had been discussing, once I was able to retire, was traveling the country in a recreational vehicle.

How that would work with the three of us was difficult to imagine. However, if I placed Rick in a group home, I would still be responsible for managing his care. And that might be difficult if we were living on the road.

What if there was an emergency and we were 3,000 miles away?

These were the cards we'd been dealt. I needed to figure out our best play that would benefit all of us. I tried not to feel resentment, wishing I didn't need to consider my brother in all my lifestyle decisions. But wasting time feeling sorry for myself would only get in the way of finding a solution.

Jeff and I had made crucial decisions before. We weren't afraid of change. We embraced it. But this change would be one that took a great deal more consideration.

"When you love someone unconditionally, you accept them for who they are, flaws and all."

—Brené Brown

The Gifts of Imperfection (2010)

Chapter Fifteen

You're Going to Live in an RV?

2011-2020, Arizona and the U.S.

In 2011, we invested $30,000 in an embroidery business, thinking the income would help support us in retirement. I guess I got the entrepreneurial spirit from my father; I'd always wanted to own a business and be in charge of my life and destiny.

Our business ultimately failed, despite our working hard for three years and trying several marketing techniques in different niches. Our single, multi-needle commercial embroidery machine couldn't compete with the larger, more established Phoenix companies with several machines. Making personalized gifts for people was enjoyable, but a formal contract with a school or sports team—groups that routinely ordered embroidered jerseys and hats—was crucial to support a business like ours. After several prospects declined a contract, we decided to call it quits. Despite losing so much money, our business failure was a blessing because we discovered we didn't want to spend all our time supporting a business. There should be more to life, we decided, than working for a paycheck.

After Jeff was forced into early retirement in 2013, we started discussing what life would look like when I could retire. We talked about our priorities, passions, and interests.

Our oldest daughter, Kelly, was busy with her life and career, and we rarely saw her.

Our grandsons lived more than 2000 miles away; Jamie had visited often before they started school. Just as my mother had compensated for her parental deficits by being a doting grandmother to my daughters, I tried to do the same with my grandsons. I constantly sewed for them. Instead of frilly dresses, I made blankets and quilts, sleepers and pants, jackets and overalls. It had become an obsession—or possibly a "manic" phase. The visits became less frequent once the boys started school, but we tried to at least visit for the major holidays. It was a depressing time for me since I couldn't be the attentive, involved grandma I longed to be—no weekend sleepovers, cookie baking, or trips to the zoo. If our retirement could have been spent with our families, we probably would have pursued different options. But we worried about becoming complacent and lazy, sitting in our recliners, watching TV while life passed us by.

After Rick had moved back to our house, our retirement decision also required consideration of my brother's welfare.

Since moving to Arizona, we loved exploring the state—discovering quaint towns, beautiful landscapes, and challenging mountain hikes. Inspired by a large coffee-table book we owned about the national parks, we decided on a life of travel. Perhaps visiting all 63 parks could be a bucket-list goal.

We decided we wanted a simpler existence that wasn't tied down to preconceived notions of a successful life—an authentic life filled with experiences instead of being attached to possessions.

Traveling the country in a recreational vehicle as full-time RVers seemed to be the answer.

The reactions to our plan from friends and family were primarily positive, but some thought we were foolish, even irresponsible. We couldn't understand how people could be so judgmental about our life decisions, when *we* would never consider telling others how *they* should live their lives. It was hurtful, but it didn't sway us. We'd always been risk-takers. Our attitude was that, if you really loved us, then you would support us. Why people think they know what's best for someone or what's in their hearts is something I will never understand. We had the belief that people should just mind their own business and worry about their own lives.

Despite believing in our plan, it wasn't easy. We had to sell many belongings and the house, and buy an RV. The logistics were daunting at times. The first step was to get out from under the accumulated debt of our failed business. Fortunately, I found an exciting job at an innovative company in Scottsdale. It was a healthcare concierge system that helped people with their healthcare decisions. It would be quite a different nursing experience; not being "hands-on" with patients was unfamiliar, but the work was rewarding, and the pay was excellent. It didn't take long to get out of debt and start saving.

Our original plan was to wait until 2017. However, delaying didn't make sense since I could retire at 62 in May of 2016. In January, we upped our game plan and started getting rid of stuff.

Modern American society has become a culture defined by consumerism. We're bombarded daily by advertising, convincing us to buy things we didn't know we needed. We've all drunk the Kool-Aid and have become a nation of hoarders, leaving us with a profoundly dysfunctional relationship with our "stuff." Jeff and I decided that our hearts didn't reside in our things or in our hopes or sense of well-being. How had we accumulated so much stuff in the first place? Why did we have five TVs? Keeping only what was necessary or meaningful to our new authentic lifestyle was liberating.

We put things in piles: throw away, give away, sell, or keep. One room, one closet, one drawer at a time. Since our HOA allowed only two garage sales per year, we needed another option. An estate auction seemed the ideal solution, allowing us to sell everything in one day.

After all the details were finalized and the house was sold, we purchased the RV and began our life on the road. It was exciting and terrifying at the same time. Since we were both retired, we had an income, albeit fixed, and could live comfortably on our Social Security and Jeff's pension alone, if we were careful with expenses. We had two savings accounts: a short-term one for emergencies and maintenance, and a long-term one (an IRA) for our exit plan if it was necessary to come off the road.

While researching full-time RV living, I discovered several blogs written by people who were already living the lifestyle. My favorite was *Chapter Three Travels,* written by Laura Greene. Laura's humorous and witty writing style had us laughing at their experiences, but we also learned valuable and necessary information. From another blog, I learned about camp-hosting, a volunteering position at national and state parks. We could work a few hours a week in exchange for a full-hook-up campsite (one that included electricity, water, and sewer). That would save us anywhere from $900 to $1200 per month, which could be added to our savings or allow for significant purchases that our fixed budget did not. We bought electric bikes and kayaks, and we installed a solar system one year. We also could splurge on spendy tourist attractions and tours, souvenirs, and meals out.

Camp-hosting a few months out of the year gave us structure and balance from the seemingly never-ending vacation. Traveling 250 to 350 miles per day to get to the next destination and staying from four to ten days in one place could be exhausting. After we were in travel mode for a few months, staying put for a while was nice. We would set up our screened enclosure next to the RV, giving us additional space where Rick could do his puzzles. It gave Jeff time to do maintenance on the rig and truck. I quickly realized that not every day needed to have jaw-dropping land-scapes or breathtaking, thrill-seeking adventures. Having some downtime to read a book or even nap was perfectly acceptable.

However, we did have some exciting adventures—zip-lining in the White Mountains of New Hampshire, a whale/dolphin boat tour in the Atlantic Ocean, and the Maid of the Mist Boat ride in Niagara Falls.

We enjoyed four incredible years that kept us gasping in awe at the most beautiful places in America: spectacular sunsets in the Grand Canyon, the foggy mist of Niagara Falls, the blue haze of the Smoky Mountains, and the surreal, ghostly pale abstract curves of the dunes in White Sands National Park. The three of us traveled in our RV from the east coast to the west coast, from the rugged, rocky Maine coast to the sugary, white sandy beaches of the Florida panhandle.

Of course, living in a small, cramped space could feel confining, but our backyard was the vast expanse of the United States. We followed the weather, staying in the southwest or southeast in the winter and the northern states in the summer. In addition to experiencing beautiful vistas and exciting adventures, we met wonderful people while on the road. These people touched our lives and connected with my brother, and we are still in contact with many, even though they live all over the country, including special friends Judy and Doug from Canada. Laura and Kevin now live in Portugal, but we still hear from them. RV life had a very positive impact on our life, and we are grateful for all the memories.

We loved our traveling life and had no plans to replace it with the more traditional existence in a "sticks and bricks" house.

Until the decision was beyond our control.

Jeff became severely short of breath as we were finishing up our volunteer gig at Topsail State Park in Florida, preparing the rig for our cross-country trip and for spending the summer on the northwest coast. We went off to a nearby urgent care, thinking

he might have pneumonia. After the intake nurse assessed him and found his oxygen-saturation levels low, she determined he needed a better-equipped emergency room and suggested one a few miles away.

Jeff was evaluated quickly with a chest X-ray, chest CT scan, EKG, and labs; he was treated with oxygen and fluids. It seemed like hours passed before the physician told us what he'd discovered. Being a retired nurse, I was familiar with the doctor's look of concern.

"There's no easy way to tell you this," he began. "You have a mass in the bronchus of your right lung. It's obstructing your airway, causing a partial collapse of the lower lobe. It's most likely cancer."

I grabbed Jeff's hand, my nurse brain going into overdrive. There was no time to break down. I had to take charge, make plans, and stay strong.

I can fall apart later.

Because it was a freestanding ER, Jeff had to be transported to the nearest hospital with an intensive care unit. The logistics were overwhelming; Rick was back in the RV at the state park, and I needed to let him know I wouldn't be back that night. But how? We were transients, with no local support system. Fortunately, I had become friends with some camp hosts and had their contact info. Rick was well-liked by all the hosts and park rangers, as he helped in the office, folding maps (a redundant job no one liked but which Rick took great pride in).

Becca, one of the camp hosts, checked in on my brother, fed him dinner, and made sure he felt comfortable alone until I came home the next day.

Since Jeff was admitted to the closest hospital in Fort Walton, I had to start the agonizing, bureaucratic transfer to a veterans hospital. Jeff was still part of the Phoenix VA Health System, and establishing him with Florida was a nightmare. One admissions counselor actually scolded me for not living in a house. She said we were extremely irresponsible and warned that his ER visit and stay at the public hospital would not be covered, even though I made the required notification in the allotted time frame. I couldn't imagine how much the hospital bills would be if the VA refused to cover this hospital admission. But I couldn't worry about finances now, not with a cancer diagnosis and dubious prognosis. The oncologist gave him two years before a probable recurrence, since the mass was inoperable.

"I'll take what I can get. I'm not done yet," Jeff told him. That's when I knew he would fight. After all, he had been a Marine. *Marines never quit, because quitters never succeed.* I had heard this from him our entire marriage.

Once Jeff was stable, he was transferred to the Gainesville Veterans Hospital, where he received excellent care. The hospital in Phoenix had a reputation for being one of the worst in the nation, and Gainesville was one of the best. I was grateful that Jeff became symptomatic before we left Florida and were on the road, thanking God for small favors. The following year was a whirlwind of appointments, grueling treatments of chemotherapy and radiation, and the difficult task of securing long-term campsites close to the hospital.

Of course, my focus was on keeping my husband alive. Jeff endured the side effects of cancer treatment, but Rick suffered from the lack of attention and inconsistent routine. And I, as the caregiver, experienced continuous guilt for failing to meet both of their needs.

Once Jeff had completed treatment, was relatively stable, and had regained some weight, it was time to make crucial life choices that would benefit us all.

I realized I needed a social network with friends, a sense of community, and helpful neighbors in case of an emergency. Rick deserved stability and attention. Jeff needed a safe, comfortable home where he could recuperate without the stress of frequently moving the RV to a different campsite.

As much as we hated to give up our nomadic, idyllic lifestyle, it was time to come off the road and settle back into a real house without wheels.

We moved to a new, culturally diverse, multi-generational development in Florida and immediately felt at home. The community had a small-town feel but was close enough to Gainesville for city amenities and Jeff's Veterans Hospital.

Moving didn't come without stress, so my attention was still not on my brother. I disregarded his moments of forgetfulness, blaming it on all the changes and disruptions our family had endured for the last three years. Finally, Jeff had an all-clear CT scan of cancer, although he had acquired chronic radiation pneumonitis, which caused respiratory distress with shortness of breath on some days. Still, we were grateful for the no-evidence-of-disease (NED) result.

It was finally Ricky's turn to get an overdue physical exam.

"One hundred and eight pounds," the medical assistant announced as Rick stepped off the scale. He was getting established with a new primary-care physician for medication refills at the University of Florida (UF) Health System.

"That can't be right," I responded. Rick had been 140 less than eight months ago. "Your scale is off."

She calibrated it once more, but the result was the same.

Now it was my brother's turn to be poked and prodded to find a reason for his unexplained weight loss when he'd had no change in appetite. A year later, after an extensive, negative workup, we still had no answers.

Then, he started exhibiting other behaviors, such as eating paper and talking to himself. His hygiene habits began to change. There were pills left in the daily-reminder compartments of his weekly pill organizer, and he was forgetting to brush his teeth with toothpaste. Rick began to wander at night, and once, I found him in the garage. The thought of him falling out there terrified me. After I was awakened at 3 a.m. to banging and crashing sounds and found Rick standing on a pile of clothes and other things from his closet, without his pajama bottoms, I couldn't be in denial any longer. I followed the acrid smell of urine to his balled-up wet sheets in the corner of his room.

He looked confused when I asked, "What are you doing?" Not responding, he seemed frozen, with a blank stare—no response, no movement. I wondered if he was experiencing some kind of seizure.

It was time to seek professional help.

"We travel not to escape life, but for life not to escape us."

—Robyn Yong

Chapter Sixteen

New Diagnosis

2023, Florida

I still called him "Ricky," his given name, but my brother had preferred the name "Rick" for years.

"Call me 'Rick,'" he'd announced when he started high school. "'Ricky' is a baby name."

I was the only one he didn't correct.

I was thinking about this while Rick and I waited to discuss his latest concerning symptoms with the neurologist. My usual go-to coping skills of distraction and denial weren't working any longer; it was time to face my brother's cognitive decline.

At 62, Rick was showing signs of dementia: forgetfulness, memory loss, and behavior changes. When the incontinence and what may have been a seizure occurred, I realized his symptoms were far too severe to ignore or excuse.

So, here we were, waiting to talk to a physician at the University of Florida Health System's Norman Fixel Institute for Neurological Diseases. This world-renowned center of neurology had recently expanded its multi-disciplinary patient-centered care to Alzheimer's disease and dementia. The center's campus was impressive, with a calm and welcoming waiting area, high ceilings, and a scenic view, symbolizing hope even when there's disease. A hallmark signature of the Institute was that every patient was evaluated for their balance and fall risk by walking across an automated gait-and-balance strip. There were rehabilitation stations for physical, occupational, and speech therapy, designed for the therapists to provide individualized, patient-specific plans. A swallowing suite to screen and prevent aspiration pneumonia is a leading clinical and research area. Finally, the outdoor physical- and occupational-therapy space included a putting green, a pond to practice casting with a fishing rod, and a healing walking path.

Rick's first consultation was with Dr. Mohiddun, an attractive young woman whose calm but direct manner was credible and trustworthy. She talked to Rick directly, looking at me only when he was unsure of the answers. Dr. Mohiddun spent more than an hour with us, getting an extensive medical history and a description of his cognitive decline and behavior changes. Lastly, she gave him a cognitive and memory test, and completed a referral for a physical- and occupational-therapy evaluation, ordered a CT scan of his brain, and scheduled a follow-up in a month.

At the second appointment, Dr. Mohiddun spoke carefully and professionally but with kindness and care.

"It's most likely middle-stage Alzheimer's disease, given the CT- and cognitive-rest results, plus his history," she said.

Although I'd researched the prevalence of Alzheimer's disease in Down syndrome adults, hearing Dr. Mohuddin confirm it was still a punch in the gut.

I stopped paying attention to her recommendations, concerns, and talk of late-stage progression. My feelings were all over the place, moving from anger to sadness. It felt like we'd been given another lousy break. I needed a new deck of cards.

Most days, I tried not to feel sorry for myself. Today, it felt justified.

"When we reach the depths of despair, only then we can look up and see the light of hope."

—Stephen Richards

Chapter Seventeen

A Very Good Day

2023-2024, Florida

"A very good day."

This was Rick's response to my question about how his day had gone at Al'z Place, an adult program that provides care for people with memory impairment and dementia.

It had been six months since Rick had been diagnosed with mid-stage Alzheimer's disease. The neurologist had recommended consistent routines and safety measures such as security-door alerts, an ID badge, and a daycare program for socialization and therapeutic activities.

Once I overcame my denial of his cognitive decline and accepted the new diagnosis, it was time to begin the navigation of Florida's bureaucracies and cut through mounds of red tape. The challenge was familiar, because I'd been my brother's advocate for most of my life, and failure wasn't an option.

First, it was important that I learn the differences between Medicare (federal health insurance for people 65 and older or people with disabilities) and Medicaid, a joint federal and state program that gives health coverage to some people with limited income and resources. Florida also has the Agency for Persons with Developmental Disabilities (APD), which Rick qualified for, due to his Down syndrome diagnosis.

I had applied for APD services in 2019, when Jeff was undergoing chemotherapy and radiation, hoping to receive some assistance to help with Rick while all my attention was focused on Jeff. Back then, I'd ended up at a dead end: There was a 10-year waiting list for services due to a lack of funding from the state. The reality of living in a "red" state that didn't prioritize marginalized groups was readily apparent.

Fortunately, I discovered the Elder Helpline, a toll-free service that connects older adults, adults with disabilities, their caregivers, and family members with support from the community. They told me that Rick, with his dual diagnosis, might qualify for a long-term care waiver from Medicaid.

After weeks of the usual red-tape runaround, I finally was able to schedule a phone assessment with the agency. But I couldn't help wondering how many other caregivers end up defeated and quit the process even before getting started. Certainly, my nursing experience was beneficial in dealing with difficult, indifferent workers and overcoming obstacles. Being respectful but assertive usually worked for me.

After answering questions for more than an hour regarding my brother's physical and mental health, his cognitive decline, and his recent behavior changes, we were approved to proceed with the next step: two home visits by an Eldercare case manager and a financial auditor from the Department of Children and Family Services—another layer of bureaucracy with an additional government office.

The first home visit went well, with the case manager agreeing that our family needed assistance and met the requirements. Completing the assessment brought something else to my attention: the profound impact Rick's decline had made on my marriage and personal mental health. Because leaving Rick home alone was unsafe, Jeff and I no longer went to the gym, rode our bikes, or had lunch dates. We shared the daily supervision and prompting of Rick's hygiene, medications, and eating habits, not leaving much time for our own interests.

Experiencing this decline had been devastating for me. Rick had gone from living relatively independently, being employed, and actively involved in his community to relying on us for assistance in his activities in daily living. Jeff's chronic medical issues and frequent doctor appointments added to our stress. When I broke down in tears in response to some of the case manager's questions, it became clear to him that we were hanging on by a mere thread.

The visit from the financial auditor was less emotional. Our income wasn't included in the determination, because I wasn't legally responsible for my brother, despite my lifelong dedication to his care. Rick's meager Social Security distribution put him below the poverty level.

Both visitors were optimistic regarding approval for the long-term care waiver. They asked what other services we would like, such as housekeeping, a home-care aide, and meals.

"Our goal is for Rick to go to Al'z Place to give him socialization and to give us a break," I told them both. "As his health deteriorates, we may need to reassess our situation. We want to keep him home for as long as possible. Placing him in a nursing home would be the very last resort; I don't think I could ever reconcile a decision to put him in an institution. It would be the ultimate failure of my life."

The next step was completing multiple pages of a medical application, a financial determination, and submitting income-verification statements. Then, it turned into the dreaded waiting game.

We started the process at the end of August but didn't hear anything until the end of December. Finally, Rick was approved for the Medicaid long-term-care waiver; however, there were still additional steps to finalize. We needed to choose a long-term care medical plan. The eldercare case manager had recommended Humana Healthy Horizons, as it was the only one contracted with Al'z Place. We waited for a Humana case manager to be assigned to Rick and another home visit, and then we waited for the daycare program to be authorized.

In the meantime, we visited Al'z Place to make sure it would be a suitable fit for Rick. The center, the consistent staff, and the university student volunteers were impressive. Al'z had a full schedule of therapeutic activities, including music therapy, physical exercise, active games, and other failure-free therapies. After completing another application, Rick was approved for a two-week trial period, three days per week, for five hours daily.

Free transportation was included with the Humana plan, but the case manager cautioned us that it wasn't very dependable and advised a backup plan, just in case. Sure enough, her warning was spot on. The service was unreliable and unsafe. The drivers were generally an hour late if they bothered to show up at all. They failed to pick Rick up at the center twice before closing; we received an urgent call to please come get him. Another time, the driver left him on the wrong side of the building, and a staff member found him wandering in the driveway. The administrator of Al'z Place recommended a low-cost transportation service through the Americans with Disabilities Act (ADA). This led to yet another application process: forms to fill out, telephone interviews, and the agonizing wait for a decision.

In this case, it was determined that our community was just outside the service area, and Rick couldn't utilize the transportation service. For me, this was the proverbial straw that broke the camel's back; we had come so far and were so close to finally receiving services. I lost it when the ADA coordinator gave me the news.

"Please," I pleaded. "We're desperate; my brother and my family need this service. We can't drive him regularly due to my husband's frequent appointments."

The coordinator's name was Millie. She listened to me vent and cry without judgment. Finally, she promised to speak to her supervisor to see if there were any options. She confided that she was the caregiver for her mother and completely understood. Her slow, southern drawl was comforting. I'd learned that, occasionally, a worker was willing to go over and above to do the right thing, if I asked.

"I have good news!" It was Millie. Her supervisor had found an overlooked policy regarding the service area we were in. Since it touched the entrance of our Arbor Greens Community, it had to include the entire community. Unable to contain my joy, I blubbered my gratitude between sobs. This loophole would never have been discovered if I hadn't expressed my desperation to Millie. The experience confirmed my never-give-up stance when it came to my brother's advocacy.

"You can start scheduling his rides tomorrow," Millie told me. "Bonnie, the scheduler, will be expecting your call."

With the transportation issue ironed out, Rick settled in at Al'z Place. The administrator there assured me Rick was adjusting well, engaging with staff, and actively participating in the activities.

Jeff and I returned to the gym, and some days, rode our bikes for extra exercise. We resumed our occasional lunch or movie dates, and I returned to my other interests, such as painting, writing, and reading, which decreased my stress.

At the six-month follow-up with Dr. Mohiddun, the neurologist, we could report positive news about the Al'z Place program and the convenience of the ADA transportation, but I also had to acknowledge that Rick was still wandering at night, and we were concerned about a potential fall. We had installed an alarm on his bedroom door that usually went off four or five times a night, so no one was getting any sleep.

The neurologist recommended Trazadone, a safe medication for elderly dementia patients and after a week, Rick began sleeping through the night.

During this same visit, the doctor recommended that we consider visiting and evaluating nursing homes once we could no longer safely keep Rick at home.

I wasn't ready to contemplate that conclusion.

For now, I wanted to enjoy one day at a time.

Very good days, indeed.

"To experience peace does not mean that your life is always blissful. It means that you are capable of tapping into a blissful state of mind amidst the normal chaos of a hectic life."

—Jill Bolte Taylor

Chapter Eighteen

New Challenges

2024, Florida

"Rick, what would you like to do today?" I asked. He was sitting at his game table where he did puzzles, but he hadn't started one yet. He was holding his ID badge from Al'z Place and an ADA bus ticket.

"Activities," he replied. "Program."

"Sweetie, it's Saturday. Your program is closed today. Let's do this new puzzle."

"No. Program," he repeated.

Rick's speech had decreased to two- or three-word sentences. As his cognitive abilities were declining, so was my patience. I tried not to show my irritation and chose my words carefully.

"I'm sorry, Rick. Your program is closed on the weekend. The nurses need a day off to care for their families, do laundry, and buy groceries."

I showed him a calendar to cross off the days until his program resumed. That seemed to appease him for a while.

He was content working on his puzzle, but I could hear him mumbling to himself. Occasionally, I heard a swear word or two: "jackass" and "bastard." It was shocking and disturbing. I had never heard Rick use such language and wondered where he had picked up this behavior.

"Rick, who are you talking to?" I asked rather sternly.

"No one."

"I heard you say bad words."

He ignored me.

He would be animated as he talked, waving his arms and shaking his finger in the air. *Was he hallucinating? And if so, who was he talking to?* I decided not to pursue it any further and made him lunch.

Rick's bedtime routine was also becoming a hassle. Jeff had more patience for some things, so he took over the supervision of Rick's hygiene. At first, he needed only prompting or reminding, but lately, he required some assistance. Rick would stand in front of the bathroom sink, holding his toothbrush, forgetting what to do.

In the morning, I picked out his clothes. He still could dress himself but often chose inappropriate items for the weather. One night, I noticed that his laundry basket was full and made a mental note to do his laundry the next day. But, when I went into his closet to retrieve his outfit for the day, the basket was empty.

"Rick, where are your dirty clothes?" I asked, showing him the empty basket.

"I don't know."

He seemed more tired that morning. I found the dirty things in his dresser drawers among the clean clothes, requiring me to wash everything. I concluded that he'd gotten up during the night and thought he needed to put his laundry away.

Was he having moments of remembering past chores? I wondered.

I had no idea how to deal with these different behaviors brought on by his dementia. His cognitive decline made reasoning impossible. We were entering uncharted territory without a map or compass. It was becoming apparent that Jeff and I needed more knowledge about the Alzheimer's-disease progression, what to expect, and how to handle some behaviors.

I found a seven-week caregiver-training course, held at the Gainesville Senior Center. The instructor was a pretty young woman who had personal experience with two great-grandparents who had Alzheimer's dementia. Amanda was a very engaging teacher who encouraged participation from the fifteen students, who had different reasons for taking the class. Three had mothers recently diagnosed with dementia; four had wives in various stages; four had husbands, while others had friends or partners with the disease. The woman who had a boyfriend with dementia was extremely annoying, always monopolizing the conservation and challenging Amanda with stupid questions. By the third week, we were all rolling our eyes and appreciated Amanda's approach for keeping the class on track.

Every week, I learned something new, understanding the three main stages of Alzheimer's disease and the behaviors associated with each one. We also learned various techniques for dealing with complex issues surrounding people with dementia.

I tried not to feel guilty as I discovered how many things we were doing wrong or that were, at least, ineffective. It was helpful to troubleshoot our individual problems with the class and teacher. We even practiced role-playing and discussed our individual coping strategies and stress-relieving methods. Amanda emphasized that, as caregivers, we needed to care for ourselves first, or we wouldn't be useful to our loved one.

It turned out that we all shared the guilt of being unable to do or be everything as caregivers, and it was cathartic to be honest with strangers when we felt most of our friends didn't understand.

The hardest class was the one describing late-stage Alzheimer's. Watching a video about a bedridden, uncommunicative, and unresponsive patient had us all teary-eyed. Listening to the quietest student talk about caring for her mother was even more depressing. It was the first time she had dared to speak. I hoped she felt better for releasing her pain and anguish.

At the last class, Amanda brought cake and ice cream and gave each of us a certificate for class completion and a copy of *The 36-Hour Day*, Nancy L. Mace's book about caring for people with dementia.

I had been considering pursuing respite care for Rick so that Jeff and I could have a few days to ourselves. Our grandson had qualified for the National Rowing competition in Sarasota, and the entire family was coming for the first week in June, which also happened to be our forty-ninth wedding anniversary. We hadn't gone anywhere without Rick in more than ten years, and we desperately needed a break. But I wasn't sure if I could overcome the guilt of leaving him in an institution, even if it were just for a week. My parents never had—how could I?

I asked Amanda and the class for their opinion. Of course, I received a resounding, "Yes, you need to go."

I called Rick's case manager, Miss Cruz, and requested respite care at Tri-County Nursing Home in Trenton. I had already toured the facility, one of two five-star nursing homes in the area, and found it acceptable. It was adequately staffed, the admissions director was impressive, and it was clean.

The respite care was approved; now I just had to figure out what to tell Rick.

I waited until the morning of his first day at the facility before I told him where we were going. I had bought a dry-erase calendar and circled the day's date and the day we'd return to pick him up. Then I explained that Jeff and I were going away to celebrate our anniversary and that he would go to a special place for his vacation. It would have fun activities, like his program had, as well as meals and snacks. I told him he'd be meeting new friends.

I didn't give him time to think about it.

"Okay—let's go," I said, picking up Rick's suitcase and heading for the car. Once we were there, the admissions director welcomed Rick and showed us to his room. Then, we met the people overseeing his care for the week. They told him about all the fun activities he'd be having and reassured me that Rick would be cared for.

Even so, it was still hard to leave. I cried all the way home and was grateful for the distraction of packing the car for our trip.

The week with our daughter and family was wonderful. Watching our oldest grandson's crew qualify for the semifinals was exciting. College recruiters were at the event and were interested in him. We were able to catch up with the other two boys as well. The middle one has already aspired to attend the Naval Academy, and the youngest is looking forward to starting high school in the fall. They are hardworking young boys, with an intense focus to succeed, because of their devoted, committed mother. Jamie is the kind of mother I wished I would have been or even had. My grandson's future looks very bright, and we couldn't be prouder.

We relaxed by the pool at our VRBO and had a romantic seafood dinner for our anniversary. The admissions director and social worker called and texted me a couple of times to let me know Rick was doing well. They appreciated how difficult it had been to leave him. By the end of the week, we felt refreshed and rejuvenated.

When I arrived at the facility to pick Rick up the following Monday, he was in the activity room, helping the director water flowers. As we walked back to his room, several staff called out to him, "Hey, Mr. Rick!"

I went to the nurses station to pick up his medications, and all the nurses said Rick had been a joy. I filled out the discharge paperwork and was told he could return anytime.

On the way home, he was more talkative than usual. "What was your favorite thing about your vacation?" I asked.

"Crafts. Bingo. Water plants," he replied.

Rick had done just fine without me.

I was beginning to believe it was possible to meet my brother's needs while meeting my own. Always putting Rick first was making me feel resentful, which wasn't good for anyone.

And it wasn't fair to the rest of my family.

"Hardships often prepare ordinary people for an extraordinary destiny."

—C. S. Lewis

Chapter Nineteen

Not a Saint or a Martyr

2024, Florida

I hate it when people call me "a saint" or say there's a "special place in heaven" for me. Or "Rick is so lucky he has you." Well, maybe that's true. But I was lucky, too.

Honestly, I have my bad days, full of feelings I'm not proud of. Usually, I try to feel grateful for the many positive aspects of my life—my husband, daughters, and grandsons. I have good health, a lovely home, and we're financially secure. I'm mostly grateful for Jeff's five-year cancer remission.

But occasionally, an ugly, jealous side emerges.

I came home from my book-club meeting upset and unsettled, which is unusual, as I normally enjoy my afternoon discussing the latest book choice with friends.

Jeff noticed. "What's wrong?" he asked.

"Oh, nothing, really," I answered. "Except everyone at the book meeting preferred to talk about their lovely vacations, European trips, and luxury cruises instead of discussing the book. I have nothing in common with these women; listening to them reminds me of our difficult life. We should be planning nice vacations in our retirement."

That was mean, I thought. *The ladies in my book club are lovely and kind. They've listened to my worries with empathy and concern. One even bought Rick special gifts for his respite week at the nursing home. And I really don't think my life is miserable. I was being ridiculous. And, of course, they had their difficulties—no life is perfect or without problems.*

For a week last month, I'd tasted life without worrying about my brother every minute when we signed up for respite care. I struggled to get back into my schedule as Rick's full-time caregiver. Comparing my life to others' wasn't in my best interest. Once I started down this rabbit hole, it was difficult to climb out.

Usually, I didn't have *time* to feel sorry for myself, as fighting for my brother's needs was necessary. I was at my best when the focus was on Rick, not myself, and I usually reveled in the challenge.

Now that we were receiving the services Rick needed, such as adult daycare, transportation, and respite care, life was more manageable. So, why was I feeling jealous of others? One of my biggest fears was becoming bitter, like my mother, and feeling contempt for people.

What is wrong with me? I thought.

Frankly, I was tired. Lately, every day had been a struggle. Not knowing what kind of mood Rick would be in when I woke him, I tried to have a positive attitude, hoping my good mood would transfer to him. But there was no guarantee this approach would have any effect.

Some mornings, he was very confused and, more often lately, after he'd stayed at the nursing home for a week. He could be argumentative and stubborn; perhaps the disruption of his routine had provoked this new disorientation. I had learned not to engage or disagree with him from a caregiver class I'd recently taken, but it could be a stressful morning when time was of the essence, and I needed to hurry him along. When Jeff and I finally got Rick dressed, toileted, fed, teeth brushed, and loaded into the ADA van, we were mentally and physically exhausted.

But then my heart would bleed when he'd come home, proudly carrying the day's art project. I knew his negative behaviors weren't his fault and that they emerged when he was feeling confused and vulnerable. For the most part, he stills gives us a lot of joy.

His Alzheimer's diagnosis had been an emotional challenge, but it had also been a financial strain. When we had a safety-risk assessment done by the Alzheimer's Association to determine potential hazards in our home, the assessor expressed concern about Rick falling when stepping over the tub and out of the shower and recommended a walk-in shower with a seat and grip bars. That set us back $15,000, although special financing allowed a twelve-month no-interest payment plan, which was doable. The remodel was necessary for Rick's safety, but I had moments of dreaming about how many cruises and vacations we could have enjoyed with fifteen grand.

I scheduled an appointment for Rick with an ear, nose, and throat specialist after his neurologist recommended a hearing evaluation. Miss Jones discovered a wax impaction. We hoped

Rick's hearing would improve once the wax was removed, but the test revealed moderate to severe hearing loss.

The next step was a hearing-aid fitting, which I dreaded, mostly because I was worried about the expense. Rick's insurance allowance was $3,600, and I was sure the hearing aids would cost several thousand more. I also wondered if Rick could wear them without losing one.

The fitting for the hearing aids went better than expected. Adam, the aid specialist, was great with my brother. Once he programmed the demo aids with Rick's hearing-test results and placed them in his ears, it was a magical transformation. Rick's face brightened with a wide smile, and his voice was a little louder than usual as he said, "Can I ask a question?"

"Of course," answered Adam.

"Are they waterproof?" asked Rick.

I almost fell out of my chair. Rick's speech had dwindled to a couple of words, and he had lately responded to any questions with a mumbled "Yes" or "No."

"Rick, can you hear me?"

"Yes," he said, nodding.

Adam said, "This is the best part of my job."

No wonder Rick had been acting out and seemed stubborn at times. The hearing loss had exacerbated his confusion, diminishing his speech to one- or two-word sentences. Perhaps this meant his recent decreased cognition wasn't as bad as we'd first thought.

Adam checked Rick's insurance benefit and discovered it would cover the entire amount of the hearing aids. He also offered to add a tethering attachment, so that, if a hearing aid fell out, Rick wouldn't lose it.

Not a Saint or a Martyr

I don't want to be a saint or a martyr, just a good sister—and a good wife, mother, and grandmother.

Learning to navigate this new path—while struggling with doing what's best for everyone and trying not to feel resentment—was certainly a challenge.

"Anger, resentment, and jealousy don't change the heart of others—they change only yours."

—Shannon Alder

Chapter Twenty

Five Years

2019-2024, Florida

We were relieved after Jeff's first all-clear CT scan. I called it "scanxiety"—the waiting period from a good result until the next scan in three months. Despite the possibility of a recurrence, we tried to remain hopeful. The best tactic seemed to simply live one day at a time and focus on the positives.

Easier said than done.

Having Rick to worry about was sometimes a good distraction.

When we decided it was time to come off the road and buy a house, we were living in the RV at the Recreation Plantation Resort in The Villages, Florida. It was the first fancy resort we had stayed at during our years of traveling. Typically, we shied away from such parks, as they were expensive, and rigs were packed in close together, like sardines. We preferred national and state parks for their natural beauty and space versus perks.

After Jeff completed chemotherapy and radiation, we had a few months before the new house would be ready—I wanted a park that had amenities and social activities and didn't care what it cost. We rented the long-term site in October for six months.

Rick and I enjoyed water aerobics; I started line-dancing lessons and joined the book club. Jeff and I learned how to play Mahjong and tried pickleball. One of the clubhouses was close enough for Rick to walk to and do his puzzles. We all enjoyed our time at the resort, meeting friendly people and learning different activities. Jeff was regaining his strength and weight. Everything was good.

On Valentine's Day, Rick and I were in the pool for our aerobics class when a woman came into the deck area, yelling for Debbie Miller.

"That's me," I said and raised my hand.

"Your husband needs you; he's in the parking lot," she told me. "Hurry."

"Go," said Janey. "I'll give Rick a ride back to your RV."

I quickly exited the pool and found Jeff sitting in his truck. He was holding a blood-soaked handkerchief and looked terrified. "I just started coughing up blood," he said.

"Should I call an ambulance?"

"No, it's calmed down some. Let's just go."

Jeff was quickly assessed at the Veterans Hospital emergency room, but the intake nurse directed us to the waiting room since he had stopped coughing.

When it started up again, he couldn't catch his breath and began gurgling with blood coming out of his mouth. I screamed for help. The nurse and doctor wheeled him back immediately. When I heard the Code Blue announced over the intercom, I knew it was for him.

An hour went by before a social worker called me back. *Oh, no,* I thought. *He must have died.*

"Mrs. Miller, I'm Mr. Thompson," he said, reaching for my hand as he directed me into a consult room.

Oh, God—this isn't good. I was trembling, trying not to burst into tears.

We sat down, and he finally said, "Your husband needed to be given CPR and placed on a breathing machine."

"I'm a retired nurse and know what a ventilator is. When can I speak to the physician?" I didn't mean to be rude, but I was so scared.

"Of course. I just wanted to explain things in simple terms. The doctors should come in shortly to speak with you."

I was relieved Jeff was still alive, but I knew this was very serious, and he was in critical condition.

Another hour went by before three physicians came in, their heads bowed. I recognized the grave looks. The brown-skinned female grabbed my hands, looked at me directly, and introduced herself as Dr. Foster, the pulmonologist. She spoke calmly, with an articulate Indian accent.

"Mrs. Miller, your husband experienced a life-threatening hemoptysis (coughing up blood) that caused a respiratory arrest. We needed to intubate him and place him on a ventilator. We were able to stop the bleeding, and he's stable but critical. He'll be transferred to the ICU soon, and you can see him there. The radiation he underwent for cancer has caused the lung tissue to be inflamed and friable, and the blood thinner he was on for atrial fibrillation contributed to the bleeding. I understand you are a nurse."

"Yes, thank you. Please be honest with me about everything, including his prognosis. I need to know the truth without sugar-coating." I tried to sound firm, but my voice quavered.

"Please save my husband. I can't lose him."

Dr. Foster then walked closer to me, put her hands on my shoulders, and said, "I will do everything I can to save your husband." I knew this was an unusual promise from a doctor, but I believed her.

Seeing Jeff sedated on the ventilator was upsetting and frightening. He didn't respond to my touch or voice but appeared comfortable, so I felt it was all right to leave, as I needed to get home to Rick. Janey had not only given him a ride back to the RV but had also fixed him lunch and dinner. She also organized five women from the aerobics class to take turns bringing Rick meals and giving him rides to the pool. It made me realize how much I needed community.

The following day, Dr. Foster performed a bronchoscopy to evaluate the bleeding source and take biopsies to rule out a cancer recurrence.

By the end of the week, Jeff was weaned off the ventilator and moved to the medical-surgical floor, but he still required oxygen to keep his oxygen saturation above 90. The discharge planner advised home oxygen, but the VA covered only tanks, which would be inconvenient. I researched portable oxygen concentrators that were the same size as a small backpack, and I purchased one from the Imogen company.

Finally, after two weeks, he was discharged, with the good news from Dr. Foster that the biopsies were negative for cancer. She concluded that the blood thinner had caused the radiation-damaged lung tissue to bleed. His lung function gradually improved with the addition of another inhaler, and he didn't require oxygen any longer.

When Dr. Foster called Jeff back to her office at the two-week hospital follow-up visit, she had tears in her eyes. She hugged him and then called him her "Miracle Man." They had developed a unique bond since she had saved his life. She gave me her personal cell-phone number and email, telling me to call or text her directly regarding any respiratory distress. I'd never experienced such personal attention from a physician; she truly was one of a kind.

Over the next two years, I contacted her when Jeff was experiencing increased shortness of breath that didn't respond to his rescue inhaler. She always got him in immediately, ordering chest X-rays or scans to determine if anything had changed. The chronic radiation pneumonitis had worsened, and he had developed a pleural effusion that was compromising his lung expansion. After she performed a thoracentesis to remove fluid, he improved quickly. Then, there was an agonizing wait for the pathology report to see if it was malignant. We've had three scares, but fortunately, all have turned out benign.

Jeff's oncologist, Dr. Rogers, is equally involved and attentive. By his third year since diagnosis, his three-month scans still showed no cancer, and two PET scans were negative for any metastasizing. She extended the interval time for checkups to six months.

This April 2024, it was five years post-diagnosis. Dr. Rogers said the current protocol allowed going to yearly CT scans, but both she and I weren't comfortable with that long of a span, so we decided to continue with six-month intervals.

The lung damage is still significant but has been relatively stable for a year. Jeff manages with two maintenance inhalers and a rescue inhaler for severe shortness of breath; he's learned to pace himself during physical activity. He never complains or stops pushing himself. I'm amazed at his tenacity; he continues to mow the yard and help with housecleaning and cooking; he recently painted our family room.

Next year, we'll celebrate fifty years of marriage. I feel like we grew up together, marrying so young and surviving many hardships. Jeff has always been my support system, prioritizing my needs before his own, like I did with my brother's. I know it wasn't easy for him to rely on me when he was weak from treatment. He prefers being the strong one who is depended on.

I read somewhere that women marry men like their fathers. While that may be true, I had my father for only fifteen years. Jeff, my father, and my grandfather are the most honorable, dependable, hard-working, loyal, kind men I've ever known. I am lucky to have had them in my life.

The most important lesson I learned from all three of them is never to give up hope.

From the day of Jeff's diagnosis and prognosis, he has never given up. And he lives each day with hope and joy.

"Learn from yesterday, live for today, hope for tomorrow. The important thing is not to stop questioning."

—Albert Einstein

Chapter Twenty-One

Divine Intervention

2024, Florida

I finally got over my pity party after the book-club meeting. Fortunately, they never last very long, due to my fear of becoming like my mother. I hate it when I get like that, and I'm sure my husband does, too. At least I can recognize and acknowledge when I'm experiencing negative feelings, but I've also learned to forgive myself for being human.

After Rick was fitted with his hearing aids, his mood and behavior improved. The caregiver-training class gave me beneficial information about dementia patients; it also recommended support groups. *Maybe it's time to connect with others who were dealing with a loved one who has Alzheimer's,* I thought.

After attending a webinar regarding Down-syndrome adults with Alzheimer's disease, I learned about a support group on Facebook and appreciated the honest feelings people shared. It's humbling to know others have the same fears, concerns, and doubts about caring for their family member. The leading group also has monthly Zoom meetings for specific caregivers, such as parents and siblings.

I attended the sibling meeting and was given helpful advice about the importance of self-care. Learning that some adults start exhibiting dementia symptoms as early as age forty, I felt grateful Rick hadn't started declining until his late fifties. Many had placed their loved ones in a nursing home because it was no longer safe to keep them home. For once, I admitted that possibility might need to be a consideration at some point.

Jeff and I had a frank talk regarding our thoughts about that scenario and what parameters we should use to evaluate a placement determination.

There haven't been any more physical declines, but Rick recently started requiring assistance bathing. We noticed he wasn't washing himself; he was just standing under the showerhead. Jeff prompted him: "Get the washcloth wet, and add soap. Now, wash your face, arms, and body." Rick could perform the tasks; he simply didn't remember to do them.

Jeff handles more daily-hygiene tasks, and I take care of the insurance details, scheduling his medical appointments, and ADA rides. It doesn't seem equitable, but Jeff reassured me it was fine. I am reminded daily how lucky I am to have this loving man in my life.

We agreed to consider our well-being and marriage by planning getaways. I booked a Caribbean cruise for our fiftieth wedding anniversary next summer and will plan a trip to New Jersey for our oldest grandson's high-school graduation.

We also discussed selling our RV, since we rarely used it. It didn't make sense to make the $200 monthly storage fee and the $800 yearly insurance if we'd gone camping only twice in the last three years. With his compromised respiratory condition, the setup, teardown, and hooking up the rig to the truck were becoming too much work for Jeff. The money made from the sale and what we would save from canceling the storage and insurance could be used for more relaxing vacations.

Since we were pleased with Rick's respite care at Tri-County Nursing Home, we decided to place him on a waiting list. Because it is a 5-star, highly rated facility, the wait time could be several months to a few years. Not knowing the rate of progression to late-stage disease, it seemed wise to be proactively prepared rather than be in denial, waiting for the inevitable.

When the admissions director of Tri-County called to offer Rick a room at their facility before he was even on the waiting list, it seemed like an unexpected coincidence.

"Debbie, this is Bo Kay at Tri-County Nursing and Rehab. We have two openings in our long-term care unit and would like to offer one to your brother, Rick."

"What? Really?" I asked. "I'd planned to call you this week to place him on the waitlist. How can this happen now?"

"Well, since he was just here, the staff really enjoyed him, and because I understand your family situation, we want to offer it to him. I realize this is sudden and may be a difficult decision, but I need to know in a couple of days. The administration wants to fill the empty beds fast."

I hung up the phone and explained the situation to Jeff. Our first thoughts were: It's too soon; we're not ready; we're doing fine. But then we discussed the possibility of another opening at this facility when we would need it. The odds were slim. After requesting input from professionals and friends who'd had experience with dementia, we decided to place him right away. There were overwhelming positive opinions about placing Rick while he could participate in activities. The consensus was that Rick's transition would be easier for all of us, and I could return to the role of loving sister instead of the resentful caregiver.

Slowly, the trepidation of placing my brother in a nursing home wore off, and the guilt lessened. Instead of just winging it by the seat of our pants, we made concrete plans and sensible decisions to benefit everyone. I felt empowered for the first time since Rick's diagnosis.

And I liked the cards we were dealt.

I called Bo Kay back and told her we'd take the room. Her administrator wanted to admit him the next day, but I had to call his Humana case manager, Al'z Place, and the ADA transportation manager. The earliest we could come was Thursday, and, fortunately, Bo Kay understood and agreed.

After breakfast on Thursday morning, I told Rick.

"I have exciting news for you, Sweetie." I tried to sound encouraging. "The special place you stayed at last month wants you to come back. They really like you. There, you could do activities every day, even on Saturday and Sunday. I know you get bored here on the weekends."

He said, "Okay." I wasn't sure if he understood. But at least he wasn't voicing any objections.

When we arrived at the facility, Bo Kay warmly welcomed us and quickly took Rick to the activities room. Everyone greeted him, "Yay! Mr. Rick is back."

Housekeeping got his room ready and unpacked his things. After we completed the paperwork, Bo Kay explained why Rick and our family held such a special place in her heart.

She had a brother with brain damage for whom she and her husband had cared for years before she had to place him in a nursing home. Her brother has since passed, but our story resonated with her.

"After Rick spent his respite week with us and was such a joy, I knew I had to get a placement for him. For his sake and yours," she said. "I was afraid you'd be reluctant to even place him on a waiting list."

Throughout my life, I have been touched by ordinary people doing extraordinary things for my brother and me. Even though I had lost any faith in organized religion, I still believe in the humanity of good people and maybe some higher power. Perhaps this was divine intervention.

We walked back to the activities room to tell Rick goodbye. He was doing a puzzle with a female resident and a staff member.

"I was here before," he told me. He remembered.

"Yes, you were. I love you, Ricky," I said as I hugged him.

"I love you, Debbie. Thank you for this place."

Jeff and I walked down the hall, holding hands, both of us tearing up.

Bo Kay met us at the door and hugged me again. "Don't worry—we will take good care of him. I promise. You made the right decision for all of you."

I believed her and knew he'd be fine.

"I have friends who do not believe in luck; they believe in blessings. Likewise, I don't believe in coincidences; I believe in miracles."

—Jane Seymour

Chapter Twenty-Two

A Wonderful Life

Florida, 2024

The first week after Rick was admitted to the nursing home felt strangely quiet, probably similar to the empty-nest experience that parents of first-year college students go through.

Since his diagnosis of Alzheimer's disease, our time has been dominated by addressing Rick's cognitive decline and meeting his daily needs. We had a few hours during the week while he was at Al'z Place. But we were constantly on edge in anticipation of further deterioration and fears of our inability to cope.

Deciding to place Rick in the nursing home now seemed to be best for all of us. Jeff and I were relieved after the smooth admission process, and Rick seemed content and pleased when we left him in the activities room, doing a puzzle.

However, the following week's visit left us full of guilt and uncertainty. As we walked down the hall, Rick exited his room, looking confused. I was happy that he recognized me, but his demeanor was concerning.

"Hi, Rick," I said, trying to sound excited. "We brought you some pictures for your room."

Jeff and I directed him back to his room to show him the family photos. He smiled slightly as he looked at snapshots of the three of us, his nephews, and our dogs, George and Teddy.

I was disappointed by the mess in his dresser drawers as I put away the extra clothes I had brought. Everything was in disarray. Dirty clothes were balled up with clean items, and underclothes were mixed up with shirts and pants. Obviously, he wasn't being supervised with his daily-hygiene activities.

I asked him how he was doing with his hearing aids, and then I noticed one was missing. Jeff found it on the floor next to his bed.

Oh, this is not good. It certainly is not what I was promised regarding his care at admission, nor is it meeting my expectations.

Immediately, I went to the nurses station and expressed my concerns with the supervisor. I was worried that, on first impression, Rick probably appeared to be functioning better than most of their residents in wheelchairs. Maybe his cognitive decline and requirement for assistance with hygiene and dressing had not been communicated to the entire staff.

"I will let the nursing assistants know," Mary assured.

"He needs assistance with everything, from brushing his teeth and taking care of his dentures, showering, picking out appropriate clothes, and placing the dirty things in the hamper. He needs help with his hearing aids." I hoped to communicate his needs assertively without sounding like I was complaining.

My 30-year nursing experience had taught me what was effective when listening to caregiver concerns versus criticizing and blaming. When nursing staff is understaffed and overworked, a negative attitude can be construed as unappreciation.

I knew I needed caution in navigating this relationship with Rick's new caregivers.

Jeff was also alarmed. "Do you want to bring him home?" he asked as we walked with Rick to the activities room.

"I don't know. What should we do?" I asked. "I'll talk to Bo Kay when she's back from vacation. She sincerely seemed to care about him."

Once we got to the activities room, the director addressed him. "Oh, Rick—*there* you are. We were going to start a game of bingo."

He smiled. "This is my sister," he told her.

A couple of residents smiled at him and said, "There's Mr. Rick. We've been waiting for you!"

Since Rick seemed more laid-back and serene, Jeff and I felt comfortable leaving him once again.

However, we had reservations about this placement decision. Of course, our guilt and perceived inadequacy came into play.

Both of us have felt the responsibility of caring for my brother, which was my priority during my entire childhood; it became Jeff's, too, after we were married.

After our six-year reprieve, when we moved to Arizona and moved Rick back in with us, our obligation has returned and has been our priority ever since.

It wasn't until Jeff's cancer diagnosis and Rick's dementia that I ever entertained the possibility of a nursing-home placement. The Alzheimer's caregiver class helped me realize that I needed to take care of myself, too. What a novel thought.

On the way home, Jeff brought up a reasonable explanation. "Maybe the staff just needs to get used to his care needs. It's only been a few days."

"True. I'm sure he gives the appearance of independence. Let's give it more time and not rush to make a rash judgment that will become more problematic. What if we can't get him back into Al'z Place, and he has no socialization?"

Later in the week, I received a letter from the nursing home, inviting me to a conference to discuss his care plan, which I eagerly accepted. At the meeting, I was introduced to a staff member from each department, including nursing, social services, activities, and food service. Each person had glowing reports regarding Rick's adjustment.

Joe, from food service, said, "I love Mr. Rick. He sits at a different table in the dining room, engaging with residents and ordering from the menu."

"He gets to choose his meals?" I asked.

"Yes, each meal has a couple of choices." Joe smiled. "I love seeing him enjoy his food."

The social services director, Diane, spoke next. "Please, bring anything you want to make his room feel personal, like placing pictures on the walls."

"I can hang pictures on the wall?" I repeated.

"Of course. Make sure you put his name on the back because we occasionally need to change rooms. We want the residents to be familiar with their room and feel at home."

Kelsey, the activities director, reported that Rick loves participating in all the activities and has made friends with Dolly. They enjoy playing games and doing puzzles together.

John, from nursing, had little to offer, since his medications had not changed.

It was my turn to discuss my concerns by addressing the dirty clothes in his dresser drawers, missing hearing aid, and lack of hygiene supervision.

One supervisor was unaware of his Alzheimer's diagnosis and dementia and knew only that he had Down syndrome. I clarified that he was once very high-functioning and relatively independent but now was in significant cognitive decline. I emphasized which activities required hands-on assistance and which ones needed only prompting.

John assured me he would convey this to the nursing assistants.

After the conference, I felt more optimistic, knowing I could attend these monthly meetings and that they acknowledged my involvement.

The following week's visit, I found him in the activities room, sitting next to Dolly, stringing beads for a bracelet.

"Hi, Rick," I said as I bent down and hugged him.

"This is my sister, everyone. Deb, this is my friend Dolly."

He seemed much happier today. We actually had a conversation about his activities, friends, and meals. He had not been this verbal for months.

I also noticed he was wearing a shirt that was not his, but I ignored it. Both he and the shirt were clean; he was wearing both hearing aids; most importantly, he was happy.

I admitted to myself that his emotional needs were being met, even far better than I could do. The structure, consistent routine, and socialization greatly benefit his overall health and well-being.

I discovered that my previous assertion—that a nursing-home placement would be my ultimate life failure—was wrong. That negative and biased thinking could have been detrimental and contribute to a faster decline.

My parents' choice against institutionalization was the right one at the time. We could provide the necessary therapy that helped him reach developmental milestones.

My decision to place him in a nursing home is the right one to meet his needs at this current time. I cannot provide the consistency and socialization his dementia requires for a healthy, safe environment.

My parents explained his Down syndrome to me when I was ten, and my father promised that our family would be devoted to giving him a wonderful life.

Looking back over the years, I believe that we did. And I'm still keeping my promise to protect my brother. As I reflect on our lives, I can't help but feel immensely blessed and grateful.

"Life is measured not by the number of breaths we take, but by the moments that take our breath away."

—Vicki Corona

We truly have had many.

Epilogue

You may be wondering why my daughters appear infrequently in my story.

I didn't include my children's lives as I wanted to stay true to the book's title and premise.

I became a mother way too young, before reconciling past abandonment and trust issues, and knew nothing about being a parent. When I returned to college, I didn't realize how difficult it would be balancing my goals and simultaneously meeting the needs of my daughters until it was too late.

It is my biggest regret, and I will take it to my grave.

But that is their story, not mine to tell.

I hope they know how incredibly proud I am and how much I love them.

I did come to forgive my mother . . . it was necessary for my healing.

Forgiving myself is not as easy.

Perhaps my girls will come to understand someday that my mother and I, both damaged souls, were simply trying to survive and remain relevant.

We did the best we knew how to.

Raising Ricky

"Your children are not your children.
They are the sons and daughters of Life's longing
    for itself.
They come through you but not from you,
And though they are with you, yet they belong not
    to you.

You may give them your love but not your thoughts,
For they have their own thoughts.
You may house their bodies but not their souls,
For their souls dwell in the house of tomorrow, which
    you cannot visit, not even in your dreams.

You may strive to be like them, but seek not to make
    them like you.
For life goes not backward nor tarries with yesterday.
You are the bows from which your children as living
    arrows are sent forth.
The Archer sees the mark upon the path of the infinite,
    and He bends you with
His might that His arrows may go swift and far.

Let your bending in the Archer's hand be for gladness;
For even as He loves the arrow that flies, so He loves
    also the bow that is stable.

—Kahlil Gibran

Final Thoughts

I'd like to share some disturbing facts. Did you know that people with Down syndrome have a 95% chance of developing Alzheimer's disease by the age of 65? Conversely, the general population has only a 12% chance of developing it.

And sadly, Alzheimer's disease is the leading cause of death in 70-80% of adults with Down syndrome. Despite these alarming numbers, there has been little research on this population.

A generation ago, the Down syndrome community helped scientists understand how genetics play a role in the development of Alzheimer's disease. People with DS are born with three copies of Chromosome 21. The Amyloid Precursor Protein gene (APP) that produces amyloid protein is located on Chromosome 21.

Since they have an extra dose of the APP gene, they have an additional amount of amyloid protein. That is why scientists believe that people with Down syndrome get Alzheimer's disease at such a high rate and a younger age than the general population.

The Down syndrome community has been waiting for more than 20 years for the pharmaceutical industry to recognize that people with Down syndrome deserve equal access to life-changing anti-amyloid drugs.

A community petition is raising awareness of this inequity to demand policy change and national attention to the systemic barriers that face people with Down syndrome and Alzheimer's. This is a huge step forward and a reason for families to hope.

Now that my brother is being cared for, my other focus will be advocating research and equity in clinical trials.

We had to fight for access to education.

Now we fight for access to treatment.

—LuMind IDSC Down Syndrome Foundation

Resources

I wanted to list some organizations that were very helpful throughout my life in enhancing my brother's life.

https://www.specialolympics.org/
https://ndss.org/
https://dsnetworkaz.org/
https://thearc.org/about-us/history/
https://www.bestbuddies.org/
https://agingresources.org/
https://www.alz.org/

Thank you for reading my book. I hope that you enjoyed it and that it touched you in any way.

I would love to hear from you if you have any thoughts or questions.

Like all authors, I rely on reviews to encourage sales. Your opinion is invaluable. Thank you very much!

—Debbie Miller

About the Author

Debbie Miller resides in Florida with her husband and continues to advocate for her brother. She visits him regularly and is very involved with his care at the long-term facility.

She is a retired nurse who has faced numerous challenges throughout her life. Drawing on her personal experiences, she has written a heartfelt story about her journey as a caregiver for her brother.

Her deep compassion and dedication extend beyond her family, and her fight is now focused on urgent inequities around new Alzheimer's disease therapies for people with Down syndrome. In bringing attention to the issue of this inequity, the community is paving the way for access to future breakthrough treatments for other diseases and conditions.

The entrenched policies we change today will improve healthcare infrastructure and make access to treatment more equitable for people with Down syndrome in the long term.